D0439196

CHINESE YANKEE

Also by the Author

Novels
Thousand Pieces of Gold
Sole Survivor
Wooden Fish Songs
The Moon Pearl
God of Luck

Non-Fiction
Chinese American Portraits:
Personal Histories 1828-1988

Juvenile
Pie-Biter

CHINESE YANKEE

A True Story From the Civil War

by Ruthanne Lum McCunn

JACKSON COUNTY LIBRARY SERVICES
MEDFORD OREGON 97501

Design Enterprises of San Francisco

Copyright © 2014 by Ruthanne Lum McCunn

All rights reserved. No part of this book may be used or reproduced in any form or by any means, mechanical or electronic, including photocopying, recording, or by any information storage and retrieval system without permission in writing from the publisher.

Library of Congress Control Number: 2014947550

Paperback Edition ISBN: 978-0-932538-96-3
ePub Edition ISBN: 978-0-932538-97-0
Kindle Edition ISBN: 978-0-932538-98-7

Author's Website:
McCunn.com

DESIGN ENTERPRISES OF SAN FRANCISCO
1007 Castro Street, San Francisco, CA 94114
Website: deofsf.com

Available to the trade from Ingram Book Company

For

Don, fearless dreamer,

Robin, bravest of the brave,

and

all my other comrades in this endeavor,

especially

Eddie Fung, Richard G. Hoover, Caroline M. H. Kraus, Gordon Kwok,

Irving Moy, Will Radell, Judy Yung

"One moment carries within it all that's gone on before."
Dreams of My Father
Barack Obama

"Everything is connected to everything else,
every story overlaps with every other story."
Leviathan
Paul Auster

"The past is never dead.
It's not even the past."
Requiem for a Nun
William Faulkner

NOTE TO THE READER

Born in Hong Kong, Ah Yee Way had no more choice in coming to America in the mid-nineteenth century than enslaved Africans. He fought in the Civil War as Thomas Sylvanus.

Chinese Yankee is his story.

CONTENTS

ONE

1854 - 1865

BEGINNINGS
1854

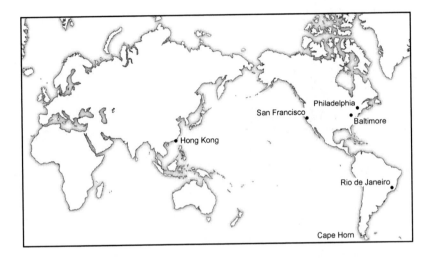

1

Ah Yee Way has lived with Mrs. McClintock as far back as he can remember, maybe all of his eight years, and there are too many tattered, sore-covered, starving urchins on Hong Kong's streets for him not to be thankful for the generous plenty she provides. Yet he can't squash his longing for family, his envy of babies snuggled in their mothers' arms, straddling their fathers' shoulders.

Pretending he's likewise enfolded in warm affection, his wanting deepens, and since Mrs. McClintock says it's impossible for a person to miss what has never been theirs, he must have once had a mother and father who loved him. Maybe brothers and sisters, too.

Sometimes parents threaten to throw away misbehaving children. *Is that what happened to me? Was I very bad? Will they take me back if I promise to be good?*

He's tried asking Mrs. McClintock whether she got him from the orphanage near the market or his parents gave him to her because they didn't want him or were too poor to feed him. But her response to his every query, "The sole parent anybody needs is our Father in Heaven," is as unyielding as her grip on his queue—

~~~

Mrs. McClintock, too weak to walk the length of the wharf unassisted, hangs on to Ah Yee Way under the pretext he might otherwise

15

become lost in the noisy, milling throngs of Chinese men who are waiting to board steerage.

The men jeer openly in their heathen tongue.

"Wah, look at that old devil woman!"

"Shame!"

"Wai, sai-loh, you a boy or a dog on a leash?"

"The foreigner's taking me to school in Philadelphia, a city in the Beautiful Country," Ah Yee Way retorts.

Scowls vanish, heads wag astonishment.

"Study hard."

"Behave."

"Bring honor to our country."

"And people."

The instructions heaped on Ah Yee Way please her. But some men start shouting that they want some of his luck. They even reach out to touch him as they would an idol!

Shrilling, "Bey hoy, make way," Mrs. McClintock jerks the boy from their wicked superstition and soldiers on, silently praying the Almighty, in His mercy, will restore her health during the long sea voyage so she can bring her enterprise to fruition for His greater glory.

~~~

At the sad-faced mite of a China boy boarding in the clutches of a shrill Yankee matron, the grizzled sailor's heart melts. His own cheerless youth surges.

Whistling, "Come cheer up my boy, 'tis to glory you steer," he gives the sad mite a sly wink then snaps a sharp salute and switches into a lively hornpipe, clenching his fists as though grabbing oars, thrusting his arms forward, sweeping them back like he's rowing.

16

His old bones creak loud as the ship's ropes, and in the sultry heat, he soon drips sweat, quits whistling. But his feet, striking the deck, keep the beat, and he pumps his arms and legs up, down, up, down in a droll exaggeration of climbing rigging.

Rewarded by peels of childish laughter, he grins and, lurching as in heavy weather, raises his right hand to his forehead, then his left, looking out to the wide Pacific beyond the vessels, large and small, plying the harbor.

The gorgon harrumphs, squelching the China boy's laughter.

Aware there'll be no befriending the mite without getting past his minder, the sailor halts and, his chest heaving, offers a winded but polite, "Thomas at your service, ma'am."

~~~

Thanks to the kindly sailor teaching him how to shift his weight from one leg to the other, Ah Yee Way has got his balance despite a belly as unsettled as the rolling sea, and he's eager to explore the ship, find Thomas. Still Mrs. McClintock insists on gripping his queue. Even for the short stretch of deck between their cabin and the ship's saloon! Embarrassed and determined to at least step over the raised threshold on his own, he tries to shake loose.

The back of his neck pricks from fingers tightening around his queue, tugging at his hair. "I know what's best for you."

Twisting around, he protests, "Let me go," and, snagging a foot on the threshold, is abruptly released, tumbles into the saloon, landing hard on knees, chin.

Hot arrows of pain blast legs and head. His eyes sting tears.

He blinks furiously. No!

"I say there!"

"What cheek!"

"Shoo, little boy! Shoo!"

Warily Ah Yee Way tips his chin up an inch or two from the rough nap of carpet on which he's sprawled, squints at shoes enormous as gunboats, trousered tree trunks, a mountainous stomach framed by flapping arms.

"Shoo!" The old bloat forms a fist, thrusts out a finger as bewhiskered lips roar, "You no belongee here!"

Too frightened to move, Ah Yee Way stares at the finger stabbing down at him.

"Below decks! You!"

A gunboat prods his shoulder. "Go!"

Mrs. McClintock's sturdy buttoned boots step alongside the pair of gunboats. "Up!"

At her command, Ah Yee Way staggers to his feet, quailing lest she throw him to the mercy of the bellowing old bloat.

"This child is in my charge," she declares to his relief while clamping a hand on each of his shoulders.

"Nonetheless, his place is with Chinese passengers below decks, not in the saloon," the old bloat retorts.

~~~

Leaning heavily on Ah Yee Way, Mrs. McClintock summons the dregs of her exhausted strength while gathering the half dozen men and two women scattered around the saloon in her gaze, offering them her most gracious smile. Then she launches into a bright explanation of the boy's name as Loyalty and Grandeur, describes how the spark of intelligence she recognized in him as an infant has since been borne out in both Chinese and English classrooms.

18

Unable to sustain her energetic beginning, she turns quietly confiding, "You see, native preachers are desperately needed for mission work in China, and I determined through prayer that Ah Yee Way, civilized and educated in a Christian nation, can lead his countrymen out of darkness, measure up to his lofty name. So I'm taking him to my own native state of Pennsylvania for that purpose, and I invite you, in the name of our Savior, to join my enterprise during our voyage. Help me arouse the boy's ambition and make him a man. Give him the opportunity to learn refinement by example, *your* example, here in the saloon."

"Yes, of course, we'll help," a young woman trills.

The portly would-be banisher of Ah Yee Way gruffly concurs and, like a dam that has burst, several more passengers accede to her request—a sign, surely, from the Almighty that He supports her enterprise and will answer her prayer.

2

The sailor Thomas has no sympathy for the ailing gorgon but plenty for Ah Yee Way, who's horribly seasick. Getting him ginger from the Chinese cook doesn't help as much as Thomas hoped. None of the usual sailors' tricks do. Not even the one he used when first at sea: Keeping a steady gaze on the horizon. But Ah Yee Way doesn't complain. He merely retches over the ship's side as needs must.

Of course, going ashore in ports of call would give the boy relief, the chance for some fun—except the gorgon, pinned to her sickbed, refuses him permission to disembark even in the company of bigwigs.

So Thomas, forgoing shore leave, spins tales for the boy, teaches him songs, how to whistle, dance jigs. Together, they make up their own ditties, sometimes singing in call and response:

"Ah Yee Way flies over the ocean."

"My Thomas flies over the sea."

~~~

In the joy of Thomas's undivided attention, Ah Yee Way crackles and bursts inside like New Year fire crackers. *This must be how it feels to have a father!*

Fixing his eye on the horizon the way Thomas showed him, Ah Yee Way builds air castles for their future together: the kindly sailor

20

quitting the sea when the ship drops anchor in Philadelphia; making a home with him and Mrs. McClintock; walking him to school; calling him, "Son."

In bed at night, he prays: *Dear Father in Heaven, give me Thomas for a father on earth. Please?*

~~~

Mrs. McClintock, further weakened by the rough passage around Cape Horn, thanks the Almighty for sending her Dr. Sylvanus Mills. Since boarding the ship as a passenger in Rio de Janeiro, the good doctor has attended her daily, easing her suffering with laudanum, flattering reports of Ah Yee Way's excellent deportment on deck and in the saloon.

She's thankful as well for the boy's faithfulness in reading the Bible out loud to her by the hour, confirming that in the fullness of time, he'll profess Jesus as Savior, ask for baptism, and fulfill her expectations for him. She struggles to accept the Almighty's will that she won't live to see it.

Every night, as Ah Yee Way kneels beside his bed, begins, "Now I lay me down the sleep," the prayer he memorized in infancy, she vows as she has for weeks, *I'll tell him soon as he finishes.*

At his "Amen," however, the words, *I'm going home to Jesus,* once again stick in her throat.

~~~

With the doctor attending Mrs. McClintock more often and longer, Ah Yee Way is ever freer. Yet he can't be glad. Not when Mrs. McClintock groans in agony and the doctor makes his skin crawl....

21

Dr. Sylvanus Mill's concerns are not for his patient, Mrs. Mc-Clintock, but his poor sister, Mary, for whom he broke his travels and is hurrying to cheer.

Thinking of her, recalling her hysteria when she was forced to marry Lemuel Duvall because she was carrying his child, Sylvanus steams anew:

Mary was just a child herself! Thirteen to Lemuel's twenty-six! Such an innocent she could not understand the necessity for a hasty wedding, leaving her childhood home, and all that was dear, to live with her tormentor as Mrs. Duvall.

Mary has confided that only their parents' gift of her beloved Mammy and a favorite slave girl saved her from complete desolation as Lemuel's bride among strangers. Then the slave girl attracted Lemuel's attentions, compelling Mary to sell her. Now Mammy is gone, too, returned to Jesus like too many of the babies Mary has birthed, and she is inconsolable.

There is nothing Sylvanus can do to restore what Mary has lost. But she was ever delighted by novelty, and he's determined to take her his patient's pigtailed curiosity—even if it means remaining on board until Philadelphia to secure the boy.

3

Dr. Sylvanus Mills—his eyes shut, chin slumped to his chest, medical journal artfully skewed across his lap as if abandoned in sleep—years ago developed this ruse for evading interaction with strangers on trains, and it's proved effective despite the pigtailed curiosity seated beside him, a curiosity that few, if any, in the packed car have likely seen in the flesh.

Maintaining the regular breathing of a man deeply asleep, Sylvanus congratulates himself for his foresight in arriving early at the depot, so they were the first to board the train for Baltimore City; his success in procuring Ah Yee Way for his own purpose by convincing Mrs. McClintock that she was too ill to persevere in her plans for the boy and he'd educate the boy on her behalf.

Of course, that fool woman's very aspirations were mistaken.

All the education any colored—Chinese, Negro, Mexican, or Indian—needs is to acknowledge and bow to a master's authority, which Ah Yee Way's been doing most satisfactorily.

As directed, he hid his queue under his cap before leaving the ship. Then, boarding the train, he hunched into the darkest corner of the carriage, dipped his chin, pulled down the cap's brim to cover slanted eyes, affect sleep. Furthermore, while the irritating soot, stinging hot cinders flying through the open windows has everyone else sneezing, coughing, and yelping, there's not been a sniffle or twitch from him.

But then the Asiatic race possesses no nerves. So the car's sway and the wheels' rhythmic clackety-clack have likely rocked Ah Yee Way into real sleep.

~~~

Ah Yee Way's throat burns from swallowing the sobs welling in waves for his kindly sailor, the sour bits of dinner shooting out of his belly. His mouth is as furred with vomit as in storms at sea—except this storm is inside him, howling: *Too late! Too late!*

There is no undoing Mrs. McClintock placing him in the charge of the doctor, who is taking him to live with a Mrs. Duvall in Baltimore City.

4

To the reverend's knowledge, Ah Yee Way is Baltimore City's sole Chinese, and with Mrs. Mary Duvall dressing her brother's exotic gift in outlandish turbans fitted with colorful stones and plumes, garish silks and satins, the curious creature draws crowds. Instantly recognizing Heaven's blessing in placing the heathen in *his* congregation, the reverend exempted the boy from the rule that restricts colored, whether freedmen or slaves, to the gallery, and both attendance at Sunday services and the church coffers these past few weeks have soared.

So when Mrs. Duvall bursts into the sanctuary, dragging Ah Yee Way and choking tearfully that within minutes of her beloved brother's departure, her bully of a husband roared, "I won't countenance a heathen under the same roof as our children. Get rid of him or I will," the reverend's distress rivals hers.

Drawing a calming breath of the sanctuary's waxy, incense laden air, he shepherds Mrs. Duvall into a pew, Ah Yee Way beside her, all the while clucking and murmuring soothingly, praying that the poor harvests of China missionaries doesn't mean this heathen will refuse baptism.

In honeyed tones that encourage affirmation, the reverend says, "Ah Yee Way, surely you want to be saved?"

~~~

Ah Yee Way wants desperately to be saved from Mrs. Duvall's fussing, her children's bullying, servants' mistrust, the gawking and poking and yapping of people who don't credit him with feelings—then restored to his kindly sailor! But that's not what he's been offered. And, paraded around Baltimore by Mrs. Duvall, he's witnessed enough slaps, horse whips cracking across the backs of colored servants, some in chains, to understand there are far harsher masters from which baptism will save him.

So he tells the reverend, "Yes, sir. I want to be saved."

~~~

"God be praised!" the reverend exults.

Mrs. Duvall drops her tear-soaked handkerchief, claps. "At your baptism, we'll replace your heathen name with a Christian. You may take my dear brother's, Sylvanus."

The heathen's eyes flash defiance. "No ma'am!"

Mrs. Duvall gasps as if struck.

The reverend clasps his hands to keep from slapping the impudent wretch, cajoles, "To be named for someone is an honor."

"I will honor Thomas, sir," the wretch proposes.

Mrs. Duvall's face crumples. "Servants take the surname of their masters," she stammers in querulous gulps. "So both you and my own boy would be Thomas Duvall. Mr. Duvall won't allow it, and Syl—"

"I want Thomas."

His rude insistence, sounding strangely more like a plaint, spurs Mrs. Duvall into renewed sobbing.

The reverend, at a loss, raises his hands in supplication to the Almighty, begins the Lord's Prayer, "Our Father..."

To his surprise, the wretch joins in, "Hallowed be Thy name," then Mrs. Duvall whimpers, "Thy will be done," and at the familiar phrase, the reverend's spirit quickens with a flash of Divine revelation: By invoking their Heavenly Master's will, the stubborn heathen and his earthly masters must accept the baptismal name Thomas Sylvanus Duvall.

~~~

At every call of "Sylvanus," Thomas flinches, vows there'll come a time when he'll be free of his enslavers. Then his kindly sailor's name will be more than in his heart and on his baptismal certificate.

REBELLION
1861
April – August

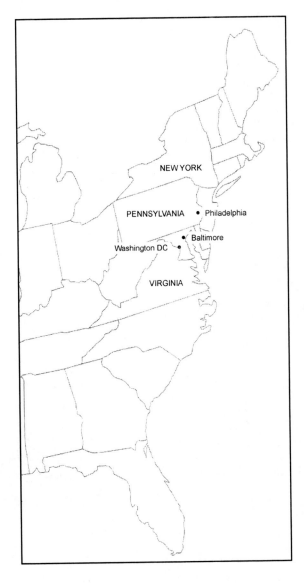

5

In his fifteenth year, Thomas trots all over Baltimore on errands for the Duvalls. Yet he's as constrained as the horses that, shackled to railroad cars by heavy collars and harnesses, haul passengers between the President and Camden Train Depots on Pratt Street's two miles of track. The street runs alongside Baltimore's inner harbor, and whenever Thomas is in the area, he slips these horses pieces of carrot he's begged from the Duvalls' cook. Even before he pets or feeds them, the horses whinny fond recognition. But their affection—whether burrowing their muzzles into his open palm or slathering his neck and face with their moist, hot breaths—only salves the worst of his loneliness. And, yearning for his kindly sailor, he steals time to go to the wharves where, raking ships' decks and rigging with his eyes, he whistles the tunes they made together, hoping against hope that at last he'll hear *his* Thomas respond.

Lighting upon a face like his own would be welcome, too: Watching Chinese disembark in San Francisco, he saw many; fewer around the docks of later ports; then, after rounding the horn, only the ship's cook; and in the years since, none except his reflection.

Maybe today he will!

Risking punishment for snagging, ripping his hated livery, Thomas vaults over hedges. Despite the crisp April air, the ridiculous turban bakes his head. The brightly colored silks cling. Moreover, they turn

31

him into an easy target for bully boys who, like the Duvalls' sons, make it their business to plague anyone colored.

Doggedly, he cuts through back alleys, narrow openings in traffic, alert for the glimmer of a dropped coin he can pocket, sidestepping smelly horse droppings and garbage. He keeps his ears cocked for talk of rebellion, increasingly fevered exchanges between peddlers, servants leaning over fences, clustered around shops, children at play.

From the rants of masters, newsboys' shouts, stealthy readings of discarded papers, he knows the election of the anti-slavery candidate Abraham Lincoln as President last November so infuriated southern states that seven seceded from the Union, forming a Confederacy. Five more have since seceded, and in his office at the Mechanics' Exchange, Mr. Duvall gloats with his clients, ardent secesh like him, that every road and telegraph between the northern states and Washington passes through Maryland, all railroads through Baltimore. So once Maryland secedes, Washington will be isolated and the Union defeated without a shot fired.

The sad surrender of Union-held Fort Sumter to the Confederacy Sunday supports that stand. But Monday, President Lincoln called for 75,000 volunteers, and thrilling whispers among colored claim some are already on their way to occupy Maryland, keep it in the Union, and free the enslaved!

The very thought of freedom from the Duvalls giving wings to his feet, Thomas barrels around a trio of pigs rooting in a heap of garbage—collides with a goat that sends him tumbling onto the pavement.

Too stunned to move, he lies where he fell, vaguely aware of the goat scuttling off, bleating indignation. Then geese flap close, honking and pecking, and Thomas, abruptly reminded of bully boys, scrambles to his feet. Hands and knees stinging, nose wrinkled in dis-

gust, he picks up his soiled turban, sets it on his head, praying his dis-
array won't be noticed, reported to the Duvalls before he has a chance
to wash.

Slimy scraps of rotted fruit, greens, and meat stick. Peeling them
off, he becomes aware of a distant rumbling, and his heart leaps.
Has the Freedom Army arrived?

He swivels on his heels, sees he's on Gay, just a block from where
it crosses Pratt. Usually bustling with laborers, sailors, and steve-
dores, the street is empty and, except for the muted rumbling, so eerily
quiet he can hear the water in the Basin slapping against the docks.

Between slaps, he picks up a high-pitched voice, two; the sound of
windows banging open; the actual words being shouted:

"Didja see the Yankee soldiers?"

"What kinda soldiers let their guns get yanked right outa their
hands?"

"Yankees!"

"I call them lily-livered cowards!"

"Huh, ain't gonna be much of a war if a coupla thousand honest
citizens hurling bricks and rocks can whup 'em."

"Blasting the cowards with their own guns is what sent them
packing!"

"They won't stop till they get home to Massachusetts, I warrant."

"The ones what got killed ain't goin nowheres."

"'Cept to hell."

Praying the women are secesh liars, Thomas hurries down Gay,
turns onto Pratt, halts: Heaped over the tracks for the railroad cars
are paving stones dug up from the street; piles of sand from upturned
carts; anchors and chains that, judging from the deep ruts, have been
dragged from the Gay Street Dock.

33

Suddenly, the clatter of hooves shatters the quiet, and Thomas, shielding his eyes from the sun's glare, glimpses a horse down by the Light Street Wharf, his harness cut, running free.

In that instant, Thomas knows he will cut loose too.

6

Thomas plans his escape carefully. By pretending he's lost a turban, selling its yards of silk, he can buy a secondhand outfit that will cloak him in his kindly sailor's protection: the tarpaulin hat, black neckerchief, red shirt, coarse trousers of a mariner. Then, every article of his disguise purchased, he'll lop off his queue, his masters' name, too, enabling him to hide in plain sight like Dr. Mills did when stealing him from Mrs. McClintock: arriving early at the depot to buy the ticket and board before anyone else; choosing a dark corner of the carriage; dipping down chin, pulling down cap to cover eyes as if blocking the light for sleep.

This time, though, the journey will be to Philadelphia and, pray God, enrollment in the Freedom Army!

~~~

The recruiting sergeant is no abolitionist. He's also not one of the fools who believe the War of the Rebellion will soon be over, the rebels defeated without a terrible bloodletting, and he foresees the day when the need for ever more men will force the Union Army to allow—even demand—coloreds in its ranks.

For months, every building in Philadelphia has been swathed in red, white, and blue bunting. The stars and stripes have hung from windows, flown from balconies and rooftops. People boast Union colors in their bonnets and neckties. Posters and banners scream: TO ARMS! GOD AND COUNTRY CALL! Volunteers flock to enroll. Still the regiment for which he's recruiting—the Eighty-first Pennsylvania Volunteer Infantry—remains several companies short of the ten required.

So, yes, he chose that morning to pretend the dark skinned, snub-nosed boy seeking enrollment in "the Freedom Army" was neither colored nor a runaway but the sailor his costume declared. Furthermore, the smooth-cheeked ragamuffin possessed the nineteen years stated on the enrollment form. The boy will need to convince others, however, and while his height of five feet four inches will likely offset the absence of whiskers and long hours of drill in blazing sun soon darken every volunteer's skin, his claim of Chinaman is bound to surprise, arouse questions.

Probably the boy recognized he was too dark to pass for white and thought—or hoped—he could find acceptance as a Chinaman. In which case, he should have added the requisite pigtail to his costume and used a Chinese name, not Thomas Sylvanus!

He did demonstrate a Chinaman's ability to fib, rolling out a seamless tale of coming to Philadelphia as a nine-year-old with his older brother and their parents, living and going to school in the Southwark District.

At the memory of this preposterous claim, the sergeant laughs anew. In thirty-six years, he's never seen a single Chinaman in the city, let alone a family, and he said as much to the pretender. At once, the boy pulled a long face, mournfully pronounced his parents and brother dead. "That's why I had to sign articles as a sailor."

Impressed by the boy's ready wit, the sergeant could not deny him. And the boy, told to raise his right hand for the oath of muster, shot his arm up in triumph, all but sang his pledge.

The sergeant checks his watch. The train carrying recruits to training must be well on its way to the regiment's camp in Easton's fairground. So makeshift is this camp that officers are housed in the town's best hotel while privates and non-commissioned officers are crammed into whitewashed cattle-and-horse sheds stinking of manure; eight to a rough-hewn, straw-covered bedstead that's about three feet off the ground. To pass in such close quarters, the boy's ready wit and glib tongue may not be enough!

PASSING

1861
August - October

NEW YORK

Easton •

PENNSYLVANIA

• Philadelphia

MARYLAND

Washington DC •

VIRGINIA

7

Thomas teeters at the open door of a shed: Pulling him across the threshold like a magnet is a gaggle of card players chatting, laughing on a bed of straw; memories of mistreatment from boys jovial with each other stay his feet.

Then, to the beat of his quaking heart, he hears his kindly sailor sing:

Come cheer up my boy, 'tis to glory you steer
To add something more to this wonderful year
To honor you're called, as a freeman not slave....

And together they prance through the doorway in a grand display of fancy footwork—only their boots scuff the dirt floor too quietly to catch anyone's attention.

Halting uncertainly, he hears: *These boys are in the Freedom Army same as you.*

"Right," he breathes and loudly announces, "Thomas Sylvanus, Chinese Yankee!"

Freckled faces, each topped with shaggy thatch, pop up as one like a toy jack-in-the box: "Yer don't look like a Chinaman." "Or a Yankee." "What are yer?"

Thankfully, the freckled three sound curious rather than accusing, and the pair of blue eyes beneath tousled black curls that have emerged beside them seem thoughtful.

41

"Our newcomer is both," the possessor of the thoughtful gaze declares. His long limbs unfold, rustling, scattering straw. "Lanky, here."

He extends his right hand, and Thomas pumps it gladly.

The final card player, a snaggle-toothed towhead, rises from the straw, chirping, "Thomas Chinese Yankee same me German Yankee."

"Well said," Lanky praises.

The freckled three chorus warm agreement, adding one on top of the other: "Our regiment's got lots of Germans." "Like Philly." "But yer the first Chinese."

"Anyway," Lanky continues, "we're all Pennsylvanians in this regiment, Philadelphians in this company."

"So what's yer district?"

"Yer street?"

"Didja go to school?"

"Which?"

Praying he'll sound convincing, Thomas plunges into the freckled three's barrage of questions. "I'm from Southwark." Since all he knows of Philadelphia is from Mrs. McClintock's homesick talk, what he saw today, he quickly adds a regretful, "But I was orphaned early and I've been at sea since, so I really don't remember much about the city or my life there."

"How long?"

"What ships?"

"Where've yer been?"

"Why dintcha join the navy?"

The last question, natural given his sailor's garb, is foolishly un-expected, the truth—*I get seasick*—impossible to admit, and Thomas flounders.

"You're the boys who say the fun's going to be on land," Lanky retorts.

42

"War is serious business," a voice scolds.

Thomas, rattled by his lapse, the sharp rebuke, peers warily into the shadowy recesses of the shed, makes out an owlish man clutching a leather-bound, gold-stamped pocket Bible who, staring at him skeptically, demands, "Are you a heathen?"

The owl's challenge cuts.

"No, sir," Thomas assures emphatically. "I'm Episcopal."

The freckled three howl: "Sir?" "Yer don't hafta sir *him*!" "He's too puffed up already!"

Thomas, his face flaming, winks as if the "sir" a joke and not a slip into a lifetime of deference to anyone white—spurring a testy sniff from the owl, more guffaws from the freckled three, a puzzled expression on the snaggle-toothed German.

"Right!" Lanky rubs his hands like everything's satisfactorily settled. "Let's have introductions!" He points to the testy owl, "That's Matthew," then tips his chin at the German, who looks to Thomas every bit as young—or younger—than his own sixteen years. "This is Jakob."

The freckled three are still chuckling and Lanky grins at them. "As for that lot, going left to right, they're Rick, Archie, and Georgi. Never mind if you can't tell them apart straight away, they're cousins and always together."

Lanky swivels on his heels, stirring up dust from the straw, yells of "Hey," "Watch yerself," "Stop," from the cousins.

Thomas, sneezing, notices a chinless redhead stretched alongside the far edge of the bed, clutching a sheaf of paper.

"That's Samuel, our lovesick groom," Lanky says. "If he's not reading and rereading letters from his bride, Millie, you can be sure he's writing her."

Lanky springs onto ground in front of Thomas, rests a hand lightly on his shoulder. "I'm an orphan, too."

43

"Is orphan same like cousin?" Jakob asks.

"No!" the cousins yelp. "Orphans don't got no ma's or pa's."

The fingers on his shoulder squeeze reassuringly, and Thomas floods with pleasure as Lanky says, "We've got each other."

Jakob's face brightens with understanding. "You *kameraden!*"

"Right, we're all comrades here," Lanky beams. "And I'll wager we're the *only* comrades with a Chinese Yankee!"

~~~

Whether in camp or town, Thomas is peppered by irksome whistles of surprise, bug-eyed stares. Yet their curiosity is only natural, and flanked by his fun-loving comrades, responding turns into a game.

To, "I've never seen anyone like you before," he quips, "Really? Neither have I."

For queries of whether he's Indian, he hops and jumps, whooping and hollering like a fool.

At demands of "You a Negro or mulatto or what?" he shifts his forage cap to the side of his head for rakish effect, purses his lips, and whistles his favorite of the songs his sailor taught him: *Yankee Doodle Dandy.*

Not until his inquisitors' "No, really, what are you?" become insistent does he stop whistling, begin singing:

"Father and I went down to camp

Along with our good captain.

There we saw the men and boys,

Including a Chinese Yankee."

Choking from laughter at the inquisitors' puzzlement, Lanky, the cousins, and Jakob chime in. So does Samuel if he's nearby sketching or painting a camp scene to send his Millie.

44

Never Matthew, who huffs, "Tomfoolery." But the cousins turn his disapproval into jokes and, together with Lanky and Jakob, emphatically correct those in camp who sneer, "Chink!" "Rat-eater!" or "Lost your pig-tail?" that he's a Chinese *Yankee*.

Thomas, quashing his disappointment at the presence of name callers in the Freedom Army, likewise joins the cousins and Lanky in jumping on those who snicker at Jakob's broken, heavily accented English, jeer, "Dutchman," reminding, "We're all Yankees here."

8

For days after the quartermaster issues their blue wool uniforms, the camp is a raucous muddle of fellows trading trousers too wide or tight at the waist, shirts and jackets too small or large at the neck, too short or long in the sleeve. But by week's end, all have uniforms that fit well enough to pass inspection. Thomas wishes his inner confusion could be as easily sorted: *Why are volunteers allowed to abuse the officers' colored servants with impunity? Why's Negro enrollment forbidden?*

As dark hued as many a Negro, he's careful never to leave the shed without donning every article of his uniform, not even when he's in the company of comrades or, cramping from poorly cooked beans, he has to dash in the middle of the night to squat at the smelly straddle-trench latrines, aptly dubbed sinks. And whether reporting for roll calls, inspections, or dress parades, he hurries to the parade ground in eager anticipation of when every soldier is standing with heels in line, knees straight though not stiff, and shoulders square, eyes fixed straight to the front.

Then, no soldier is distinguishable from another in his row, his squad, his company, his regiment, and for as long as he's in this sea of blue, his inner turmoil calms, he feels the bliss of absolute belonging.

~~~

Between the bugle calls for reveille at five every morning and lights out at nine in the evening are seven hours of drill, and Thomas, his feet painfully blistered from breaking in regulation metal-heel-plated shoes, joins in his comrades' grousing and growling with utmost sincerity. Yet he also savors the relief those hours provide from the vigilance necessary for passing as an orphaned sailor.

Thankfully his Yankee accent, acquired from Mrs. McClintock, requires no thought and Lanky skillfully deflects any quizzing for details about how either of them was orphaned. Even so, close attention is required for the most casual exchanges, and he's constantly racking his memory for details about shipboard duties and ports of call, keeping his ears peeled no matter where he goes—including the smelly sinks—for information about Philadelphia that he can use.

Exhausted long before the final isolated bugle note sounds for lights out, he welcomes the sweet release of sleep. His last thought, more a prayer, is that by the time the regiment leaves for Washington, he'll be as well versed in his stories as soldiering. Then maybe he can be more at ease. Like his new comrades.

9

O to enjoy Thomas's fluency and Yankee accent, ease with Amerika, Amerikans, Jakob sighs. Their temporary camp on Washington's Kendall Green holds many regiments, and its acres of white bell-shaped tents are adorned with patriotic charcoal sketches, paintings, and mottoes that even students from the adjacent Columbia Institution for the Deaf—faces bright, fingers flying—obviously relish but would remain a mystery for him if Thomas or Lanky didn't explain.

So his kameraden won't think him a complete dummkoph, Jakob doesn't always ask about what puzzles him. Such as when Samuel wanted to draw the freedom goddess on their tent and Matthew objected to it as unchristian yet accepted Lanky's suggestion of an eagle, the Roman gods' sacred animal.

A fierce eagle is better than a pretty goddess. Painted in lifelike colors, Samuel's bird scowls as fiercely as the gilded eagles atop every regimental flagstaff. At the cousins' urging, their eagle's beak even drips blood, and clutched in its talons is a banner that proclaims what they're fighting for: FREEDOM AND RIGHT.

~~~

Freedom and right? Nothing's right! Matthew fumes. When enlisting at his church's altar under the banner, "What God hath joined, let no man put asunder," he anticipated serving alongside fellow congregants. Instead, he's tenting with an appeaser; lovesick painter; sly Chinaman; thick-headed, thick-tongued Dutchman; and three rowdies as troublesome as the errant pigs that they, as hog reeves, used to weed from the well-mannered herds responsible for eating the garbage in Philadelphia's streets and parks.

For refuge, he turns to his Bible—winces as he eases it from his pocket. Gingerly, he sets it on his lap, blows on fingers and palms tender from blisters upon blisters.

Glorying in the brass band and cheers that greeted their regiment's arrival to defend the capital, he never imagined their duty would be shoveling dirt like common laborers. Truly, he's as beset as Job.

~~~

Thomas doesn't like the new camp overlooking Washington's Navy Yard any better than his comrades. Dense plumes of black smoke never stop belting from the Yard's iron foundry and copper rolling mill, so soot grimes their tents, uniforms, skin. The smoke *does* hide the sun, though. Whereas, here, at the fort where the regiment is building earthworks, hot sun strikes full force through the gritty haze thrown up by their shovels, and his chest heaves, itchy rivulets of sweat drip from every pore, his eyes sting, his nose runs. Willing to endure any discomfort to protect the Union's capital and trounce the Confederacy, he nonetheless maintains a steady rhythm.

On his right, Samuel drags ever slower, grumbling, "The rebs have thousands of slaves to do *their* digging."

Thomas tenses.

Matthew halts work altogether. "*We've* got runaways."

Have I betrayed myself in talk? Sleep? Head and belly churning, Thomas keeps plunging shovel into dirt, adding to the pile over his shoulder.

"Matthew! Matthew! Matthew!" the cousins jibe in unison.

"Dontcha get it?"

"Them runaways ain't slaves no more."

"Cuz Massa Abraham's got us for slaves."

"Don't be disrespectful of our President," Matthew scolds, taking up his shovel.

"All I meant is runaways benefiting from Union protection as contrabands of war ought to do their share."

"Contrabands cook and wash," Jakob protests.

Matthew snorts. "They ought to—"

"The only oughta is we oughta be fighting the Johnnies stead of digging," Lanky cuts in.

This is one of the rare bones Matthew, Jakob, and the cousins have gnawed on before in harmony, and they pounce soon as Lanky throws it. Thomas, though, can't stop fretting.

Only fugitives from Confederate labor battalions are protected under the law as contrabands of war, and slavers are issued official passes to enter Union camps and search for runaways. In fact, slavers are allowed to take possession of *any* colored person they proclaim a runaway, so he can as easily be plucked again for servitude against his will as when Dr. Mills took him from Mrs. McClintock. And the brag of their colonel's servant, "Our colonel won't let no slaver into our camp lessen he lose me," offers thin comfort. Since guards are drawn from every regiment in camp, a soldier posted at the gate could be under one of the many officers who've declared their intention to cooperate fully with slavers on grounds the war isn't over slavery but Union.

Thomas is certain of his comrades' support for Union, but where they stand on slavery is unclear despite the motto "FREEDOM AND RIGHT" on their tent.

He wants to think Samuel's grumbling stemmed from nothing more than fingers too blistered to hold a pencil for writing his Millie;

Matthew's his snobbery. The cousins will say anything to goad him, Lanky to make peace. As for Jakob—

Thomas grabs a pick-axe to break new ground: Never mind where others, including his comrades, stand; *his* war is to end slavery, and if he's delivered up to a slave catcher, forced back into servitude, he'll run again.

GUNNING
1861
November

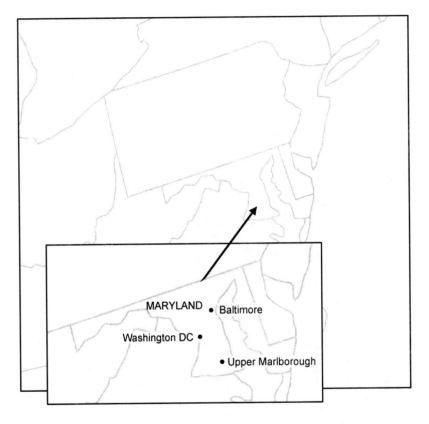

MARYLAND   • Baltimore

Washington DC •

• Upper Marlborough

10

Hurrying through the camp's cold, dark streets with Lanky, Jakob's head throbs. Inside every lantern-lit tent, silhouettes are busily bobbing up and down. His own knapsack and haversack packed, he's ready for tomorrow's departure. But try as he might, he can't understand their regiment's orders. He only knows that since the orders, the cousins have been afire with excitement, Thomas strangely jittery.

Finally, Jakob's bewilderment bursts out, "Lanky, why we go guard Maryland polls in election?"

"The state's full of rebels, see, and if *their* candidates for assembly and Governor win in the election, Maryland will leave the Union and join the Confederacy. Then Washington will be cut off from the rest of the Union. So we have to make sure the Union Party wins."

"How?

"We'll make any man who comes to the polls swear loyalty to the Union before we let him vote."

Astonished, Jakob gasps, "Rebel make oath?"

Laughter explodes. *The cousins! Where are they? What's the joke?*

Shouting, "Halt," the three jump out of the dark.

Jakob blinks. No, the cousins aren't aiming rifles at him and Lanky but their right arms, extended with fingers positioned like boys playing at holding guns!

"Yer wanna vote?" Rick demands.

Thoroughly confused, Jakob stutters, "Vas?"

"Foreigners can't vote," Rick declares.

"I'm American and over twenty-one," Lanky retorts cheerfully.

"First, yer gotta swear allegiance to the Union on the Bible," Georgi orders and mimes holding up a book while Rick pokes his pretend gun into Lanky's chest.

"Never!" Lanky rasps through splutters of laughter.

Rick stabs Lanky's chest repeatedly. "No oath, no vote!"

"Now do yer see, Jakob? We gonna make them swear by gunning," Archie crows.

As Lanky's choked ha-ha-ha crescendos into a roar that rivals the cousins', Jakob nods. He *can* see his kameraden are play-acting. And, since Amerika is a demokratie, they *must* be joking. So he stretches his lips into a big smile, hiding behind silence his failure to understand the joke, how the regiment's going to ensure the Union Party wins, what it is about going to guard the polls in Maryland that's got Thomas so jumpy.

~~~

Silence after lights out strictly enforced, no one speaks. Spooned together for warmth, however, Thomas feels his comrades' every ragged breath, restless twitch, hopes they can't hear his heart drumming hard as when he was fleeing Baltimore.

Soon as reveille sounds at two, they roil into activity. In the pitchy dark, Matthew prays out loud for the success of their Holy Crusade. The cousins, falling over everybody like yappy puppies, untangle their pants, tug on their shoes. Throwing open the tent flap, they let in icy, refreshing air, head out for the sinks, Jakob, Samuel, and Lanky hard on their heels.

Thomas has been praying for success, too, but silently, and while shaking off the blanket, groping for his shoes. Yanking one on, he adds a fervent plea: *Send us to guard polls far from Baltimore.*

Realizing his left shoe's on his right foot, he switches. Fingers fumble as he laces, and he comes out wrong, starts over—once, twice, then the other foot, becoming ever more heated. Finally done, he lurches into the cold, crunching across frost so thick and white it might be snow.

Since the lines at the sinks are bound to be long, many a soldier is taking advantage of the dark to piss or squat behind heaps of garbage to avoid the wait. He doesn't, and by the time he leaves the sinks' slippery stink, the camp is warming from cheerful cooking fires.

Competing with excited chatter, the clank of buckets and pans is the welcome sound from hundreds, thousands of rifle butts smashing coffee beans, releasing their rich aroma. Hot coffee and the delicious sizzle of scrapple call, but he notices an aide, satchel bulging, galloping into camp. *Bringing new orders?*

The possibility trumps coffee, Samuel's mouth-watering scrapple, and Thomas chases over to the tents where the regiments' officers are quartered, gives their servants a friendly helping hand as they step in and out with steaming platters, coffee pots.

Chitter-chattering as well, he learns the postings for each regiment have arrived. The Eighty-first's ten companies will be guarding different polls. His, Company D, will be in Upper Marlborough.

To be far from Baltimore *and* under the sole command of their captain—a staunch abolitionist—will lessen his risk of recapture considerably, and Thomas, racing back to his comrades, breathes a fervent prayer of thanks.

Breakfast over, Jakob's begun yanking their tent pegs, but a rushing northwest wind is whipping the canvas. Thomas dives in to help, and with Lanky shouting above the cousins' bellowing, Matthew and

Samuel stepping lively, they roll the tent, hurriedly load the wagons. Overhead, clouds plump with rain roll in. As they sling knapsacks and blanket rolls onto their backs, shoulder their muskets, thunder growls. Marching out of camp, the clouds burst.

For the next two days, sheets of black, sleety rain drench all to the skin, set teeth to chattering, and turn the roads into gooey red and yellow rivers. Mud-caked shoes, soggy, ice-cold tunics and pants drag at benumbed limbs. The rolled blankets and knapsacks on their backs double, treble in weight. But Thomas fairly bursts with pride. Less than three months ago, he was a defenseless slave running north. Now he's returning an armed Union soldier responsible for policing polls.

~~~

The captain's plan for a Union victory at the polls is simple.

Government ballots are bright yellow. So he posts parallel rows of armed soldiers at the entrance to each poll, orders voters to walk between them holding their ballots, his men to turn away anyone with a color other than yellow. Not one secesh dares assay the armed gauntlet, and many a soldier, robbed of the chance to fire his gun at the enemy, is mad as the devil. But the captain's well pleased: There'll be no more bloodless victories once the "balls" begin.

THE BALL
1862
January – June
ACTIVE OPERATIONS
PENINSULA CAMPAIGN

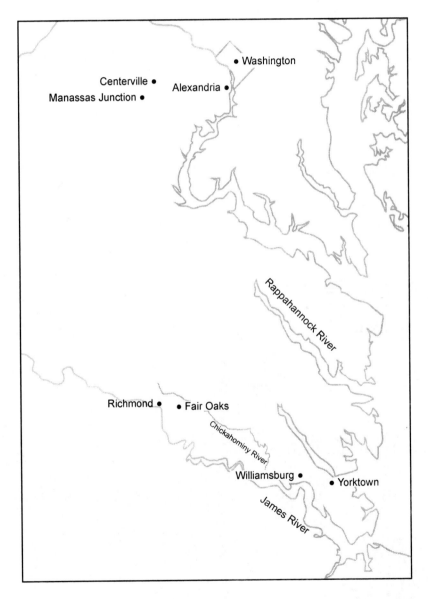

• Washington

Centerville •
Alexandria •
Manassas Junction •

Rappahannock River

Richmond • • Fair Oaks

Chickahominy River

Williamsburg •
• Yorktown

James River

11

In the brigade's winter camp a few miles from Alexandria, hard snow grates and cracks under shoes, bone-chilling gales gust through tent seams. There's no fear of slave catchers in this weather. But even huddled by the stove with his overcoat on, Thomas can't stop his teeth from chattering, and at the open-trench latrines, his bared skin freezes; every breath hurts.

His feet and hands, however, are snug in woolen socks and mittens knitted by the cousins' mothers. So are Lanky's. They both enjoy gifts from their comrades' families—sweet jams from Samuel's Millie, thick slices of spicy fat sausages from Jakob's mother, slivers of tasty cakes from Matthew's sister.

To repay their generosity with falsehoods shames Thomas, and his daily prayer is for the fight to begin, the war to be won, so he can speak and live freely.

~~~

Thomas hasn't forgotten the Union Army's humiliating routs by Baltimore's citizens and in battle against the Confederate Army before he ran north. But he and his comrades in no way resemble the raw, untrained troops who skedaddled from the rebels.

On sunny days, the entire brigade drills on ground especially cleared for that purpose, and the gilded eagles atop flagstaffs, the officers' gold braids, shoulder straps, and sword hilts gleam. The polished brass buttons on every uniform glitter like jewels.

As the drums roll, the six regiments, each with their own proud colors flying alongside the national flag, form into line of battle. They advance, wheel, break into columns, and then reform for more maneuvers.

Thrilling to their individual and collective precision, he thinks of dancers, understands why officers call battles "balls."

~~~

Near the end of February, the brigadier at last promises "a ball some time today." Each soldier is issued three days' rations for their haversacks, forty rounds of ammunition for their cartridge boxes, and ordered to hold in readiness to march at ten minutes' notice.

Thomas, fingers atremble from nervous excitement as much as cold, polishes his already shiny gun. The cousins jump up and down hollering, "We gonna gun rebs!" "Shoot 'em dead!" "Yeah!" Matthew takes out his Bible, studies his sister's inscription on the flyleaf. Samuel writes a letter to his Millie, slips it under the ribbon holding hers. Lanky dashes back and forth to the sinks. Jakob repeatedly quizzes him, every passerby: "Order come for march?"

At ten o'clock, a battery of artillery clatters through the camp fast as six horses can drag each gun through mud. Jakob and the cousins fret the ball will be over before they get to it. Thomas prays for victory. Lanky makes another dash to the sinks.

At one o'clock, the brigade finally assembles in sleety rain for a farewell address from the brigadier general, prayers from each regiment's chaplain. So long winded are they that by the final Amen, Thomas has frozen into an unfeeling block.

Then the band strikes up the *Song for Battle,* and as the notes pulse through his spine, the words sound in his heart:

Oh comrades, going forth to battle,

Forget to doubt—forget to fear;

Let step be firm and eye be clear...

But the command at song's end isn't to march. They're to go back to their posts and hold ready to move on a double-quick at the sound of the bugle!

Waiting, Thomas endures moments that are hours, hours that are days.

Close to midnight comes word, "There'll be no ball."

~~~

The cousins make straw-stuffed effigies of Johnny Reb for them to shoot, and Thomas, taking aim, pictures slave catchers.

The real Johnnies, holed up in Manassas, humbug Union generals by replacing their cannon with painted logs that resemble cannon barrels, slip away unnoticed.

Belatedly alerted to the Johnnies' disappearance by greasy black clouds of smoke, Union generals send the regiment to chase the scoundrels, and Thomas, setting out, tingles with renewed anticipation. The cousins strut like cocks.

All agree: The Johnnies are on the run!

Only the cowards keep burning bridges in their wake, so temporary bridges have to be built, and cutting trees the right length is no easy business, especially for Matthew, who has no talent for wielding axe or saw. Floating the cut logs, placing them in position while standing up to armpits in water can't be hurried either, and by the time a bridge is finally built and crossed, nothing is left of the scoundrels except their tracks in red Dixie mud—their tracks and acrid ash and smoke billowing from yet another bridge that must be rebuilt.

12

The day the regiment's recalled from bridge building for a campaign in the Peninsula, Thomas is certain their huzzahs can be heard as far away as Richmond, the rebel capital they mean to reclaim for the Union. As the fleet carrying the Army of the Potomac plies the brilliant blue water of Chesapeake Bay in double columns, lively music from regimental bands, joyful cheering, shouting, and joking on deck and between vessels make him feel he's won a coveted invitation to a picnic, an affair far more glorious than the Sunday school outings in Baltimore from which he used to be excluded.

To avoid notice from strangers in other regiments, quizzing, possible eviction, even—pray God, no!—return to enslavement, he's stuck close to his comrades, positioned his forage cap so the bill shadows his eyes, the bridge of his nose. As the deck rises and falls, however, his belly does, too, reminding him of his voyage from Hong Kong, its dark end. Gulping, he jumps to subdue his queasiness by joining the hearty singing:

"In freedom's name our blades we draw,
She arms us for the fight;
For liberty and right,
The Union must, shall be preserved."

~~~

At Fair Oaks their colonel shouts, "We've wanted a fight. Now we've got it. Show them what we're made of!"

Thomas, in line of battle with his comrades, vows, *I will,* adds his voice to the regiment's hurrahs for the Union, the cousins' stout declarations, "Philly won't be ashamed of us!"

The initial volleys fired on both sides sound as satisfyingly precise as at drill. But as they advance, volleys are punctuated by disturbing screams and cries, thugs of bullets sinking into flesh, crumpling bodies blossoming blood. Black smoke from repeated volleys billow, shrouding the battlefield which, unlike their beautifully cleared drill grounds, is dense pine forest and underbrush riddled with creeks and bogs, deep mud puddles from days of heavy rain.

In the muck and smoke, battle lines quickly crumble. Orders change accordingly. Obeying best he can, Thomas loses sight of his comrades, but hears a shout, "Looky here, mind how you shoot!"

Who? Me?

"I am!"

His response is lost to the boom of cannon. The very ground beneath them shakes. Then, despite the crash of musketry, pounding hooves, his heart, he catches Lanky and Jakob calling out to each other, the cousins' yells and shrieks:

"Just keep cool will yer?"

"That ball dint miss my head two inches!"

"I got better sense than to shoot yer."

"There tumbles another."

"Give it to 'em!"

Their captain staggers. *Shot?*

No. He's stooped below the smoke bank, his head cocked like a hunting dog seeking its quarry.

Straightening, he orders, "Fire at will," and Thomas loads and fires, then presses forward, dodging thrumming bullets thick as bees.

Shells screech. Limbs snap, splinter in showers of twigs and leaves, bone, flesh, and blood. His eyes stinging from dirt, acrid clouds of choking smoke, he squints, coughs. No face, sweaty and black from powder, is recognizable. In the sulfurous haze, he can't distinguish filthy blue from filthy gray. Even so, relying on glimpses of colors for guidance, he advances. He loads and fires.

Suddenly, even stooping, he can't find either friendly stars and stripes or the foe's stars and bars. Yet the hail of lead, furious clank and clang of steel ramrods thrust into rifle barrels hasn't stopped, and the pit of his belly sinks. Automatically he tears open another cartridge with his teeth, licks the gritty powder graining lips, swallows, but has no spit left to wash away the bitter taste. His fingers—sweaty as his throat is dry—almost lose the ball they're trying to slide into the smoking, blistering hot barrel.

Gripping the ramrod extra tight, Thomas shoves panic down along with the cartridge paper for wadding. He cocks the hammer, draws a percussion cap from his pouch, places it on the cone, jerks the rifle to his shoulder.

Unable to see, he rubs his eyes. Powder from his fingers burns like pepper. Tears stream. A bullet whistles past his ear. Instinctively, his finger pulls the trigger.

The butt of his rifle ratchets against his shoulder, the scent of burnt powder sears his nostrils. Coughing, he fumbles for another cartridge....

FIGHTS
1862
June
PENINSULA CAMPAIGN

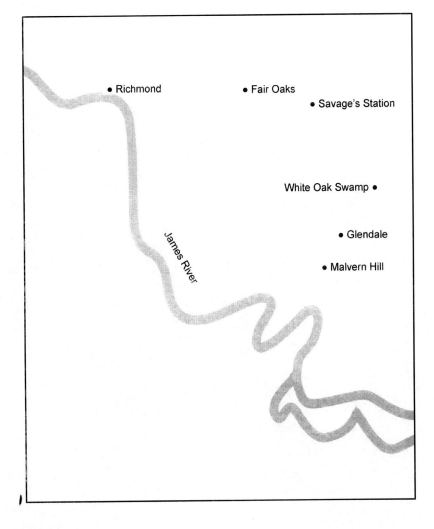

13

Awake or asleep, Thomas is haunted by the corpses in the long rows of individual graves in which he and his comrades laid the Union dead, the massive pits in which they tipped the enemy's. Then as now, friend or foe, bodies shattered or whole, faces twisted in terror or no, insects roam in and out of nostrils, eat at eyes, tunnel into ears, mouths....

Their own mouths and noses masked by kerchiefs to muffle the stink of rotting flesh, neither he nor his comrades spoke except as necessary while laboring in the burial detail.

None of them have said a word about their grisly duty since.

And they don't speak now as, pitching in to help Samuel retrieve the papers flying from his dropped knapsack, they pick up sketch upon sketch of anguished faces, ruined bodies.

~~~

His guts cramping and twisting, Lanky thrusts the sketches he's gathered into his nearest comrade's hands and staggers, doubled over, in search of the nearest place he can decently squat.

In their regiment, the number of wounded and dead from the Battle of Fair Oaks exceeded an entire company; for the Armies of the Potomac and Virginia, the count will doubtless run into the thousands! And every person who supports the war—in particular those who take

71

up arms—bears responsibility for casualties. So he was taught from birth and—despite disownment by family, the Society of Friends—still believes.

His very bowels revolt against the carnage. But Slavery, having seized the sword, can only perish by the sword. So fight he must.

~~~

Each time a drum roll order sounds to form lines of battle, Thomas and his comrades grab their rifles, and whether in a skirmish or battle, they fight like tigers.

Hardly a day or night passes without the long roll beaten, often more than once, and as the regiment tramps to one murderous fight after another, the gunning, marching, snatched moments of rest bleed together. Fiendish yells, musketry, the shrieks and screams of shells never stop resounding in his head. Neither do the frantic brays and whinnying of mules and horses kicking, streaming every which way on the gallop. The stink of burnt powder and death is always in his nostrils. Exhaustion as much as sulfurous smoke and cannonading sting his eyes, rock the ground beneath his feet.

~~~

Through a shroud of lingering battle smoke, Thomas squints blearily at Negro guides leading trains of wagons, artillery, caissons, and troops into deepening dusk, dark woods.

No drums beat or bands play. Regimental colors are furled to the staffs. Since artillery and wagon trains have right of way, worn men march as best they can in columns of four on either side. The less seriously wounded limp after the surging throng. Some are supported by comrades. Others lean on sticks, improvised crutches.

At their painful staggering, the cries of men in ambulances leaking blood, the sobbed entreaties of the thousands of wounded about to be abandoned, Thomas's heart wrenches. *Must they be left behind?*

"They'd slow us down from getting to our next fight."

Matthew's response startles. *Did I speak out loud?*

Horrified he might have unwittingly dropped his guard, Thomas struggles to blinder his eyes, to block his ears against all except commands.

~~~

In the inky blackness that Thomas associates with midnight, loud rumbles of thunder crack the sky, blinding jags of lightning rip loose a storm. Fumbling for his rubber blanket, he grimly wraps his musket, protecting it—not any of the groaning huddles of wounded collapsed by the wayside—from the downpour.

To his relief, the road of pale sand does not turn slippery in the rain, but hardens. It even remains eerily visible with the aid of pine torches—as if the wagons and men, the teamsters' yells and curses, their cracking whips and their beasts' pained protests were a theatrical.

Thomas sighs wistfully.

When attending the theatricals staged in winter camp by actors in the brigade's New York regiments, he could count on a show unfolding as the master of ceremonies promised. But the final battle, which the general vowed was "at hand" weeks ago, has yet to happen. And officers have insisted, "Just another fight or two and we'll be in Richmond," far too often for him to credit.

According to Lanky, they aren't even headed for the rebel capital but retreating to the protection of Union gunboats on the James River.

As if trying to convince themselves, the cousins counter:

"We ain't turned our backs on the Johnnies."

"Yeah, we been facing and fighting them."

"Beating them, too!"

"Not quite," Matthew says. "We've no clear victories. But we're not retreating. We're laying a trap."

~~~

Rations irregular, cooking fires nigh impossible because of constant fighting and marching, Samuel can scarce manage planting one weary foot in front of his other.

Had he the energy to join in the talk, though, he'd point out to Matthew that since provosts on both sides always patrol a battle's perimeters, cracking whips at would-be skedaddlers, driving them back into the fight, every soldier is in a trap.

TRAPPED
July 1862 – May 1863

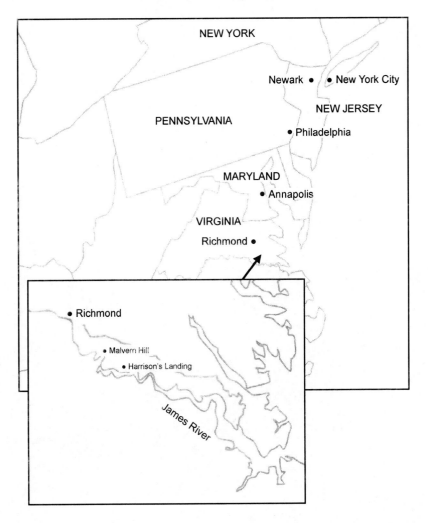

14

Thomas, weighed down by defeat as much as exhaustion, drags into the muddy camp at Harrison's Landing with his comrades, the remains of the Army of the Potomac.

Nearing sutlers touting Northern papers like city newsboys, he hears: SEVEN DAYS' BATTLES COMPLETE SUCCESS! OVERWHELMING DEFEAT OF THE ENEMY! And his spirits lighten.

The commanding general, in a proclamation praising the army's valorous conduct, confirms: "Under every disadvantage of numbers, and necessarily of position also, you have in every conflict beaten back your foes with enormous slaughter."

SEE, the cousins and Matthew gloat in rare union.

But the newspapers and general don't explain—and his comrades can't—what exactly the costly victories have accomplished. Or why the army seems trapped in enemy territory without enough surgeons for the thousands—some say tens of thousands—of desperately wounded.

~~~

In the field, the surgeon dulls his senses with whiskey until he can turn his back on soldiers mewling, twitching for help but can't be saved because of heads partially shot away or bodies ripped open, shattering vital organs. Then he saws, probes, and stitches together those who might live, many as they groan, shriek, curse, or pray aloud.

He's so practiced at amputation that in less than ten minutes, he can excise a limb, tie off arteries, scrape the end of bone smooth, and cover all neatly with a flap of skin he stitches closed, leaving a hole for drainage. Operating hour after hour without rest, though, he sometimes has to lean against the amputating bench to keep from fainting. Once, poking around a chest cavity for splinters of shattered bone while under heavy cannonading, he shut his eyes to focus his concentration—fell asleep. And although two weeks have passed since the regiment's last battle, the demand for surgeries hasn't abated. So whether cutting into flesh and bone, peeling off blood- and puss-stiff bandages, cleaning stumps crawling with maggots, slicing off green-black bits stinking of gangrene, patching, or prescribing, he has to labor against nodding off.

As he assures the Chinaman fretting over blurry vision, "My own sight is impaired by exhaustion. Not just yours. I'll give you an excuse from guard and fatigue duties so you can rest."

~~~

Thomas wants to believe he's no more bleary-eyed than during long days and nights of marching and fighting.

But rest doesn't lead to improvement.

His eyelids, puffy and tender, hurt horribly when touched.

Yet touch he must: Unless wiped repeatedly with a rag, his eyes puddle, weep streams.

The cousins joke about crocodile tears. Lanky talks Samuel into lending him Millie's soft lawn kerchief. Matthew suggests more thorough washing. Jakob fetches fresh water from the river.

Still Thomas feels his eyelids swell. His field of vision shrinks.

Then his eyes start oozing something thicker than tears, become so crusty and painful, he can't bear to do more than dab at them. He stumbles over knapsacks, buckets, tent pegs.

The cousins stop joking, rally to his aid, taking turns, along with the rest of his comrades, to accompany him, so he won't fall, lose his way.

Convinced something is seriously wrong, he tells them, "I have to go back to the surgeon."

Lanky, suffering horribly from the flux, says, "I'll go with you."

~~~

Waiting in line, they roast for hours under a blistering sun, fighting off buzzing flies, whining mosquitoes.

Lanky groans, "Anyone who isn't already sick *will* be."

Finally inside, they both gasp at the stale reek of alcohol.

"The man should be stripped of a surgeon's green sash!" Lanky exclaims.

All Thomas wants is for the live coals in his head to stop burning.

"You've been attacked by a disease of the eyes," the surgeon slurs. "Maybe brought on by smoke from powder. More likely, the blast or fumes from an exploding shell."

~~~

Thomas's comrades rehash the regiment's most severe fights in the past month one by one, conclude he could have been affected by smoke, powder, fumes, exploding shells at Fair Oaks, Savage's Station, White Oak Swamp, Glendale, or Malvern Hill—or all.

The surgeon, far less thorough in his examinations, is as vague in determining a remedy. Not just for him but for Lanky, shuffling ever more feebly to the sinks.

With no other recourse, Thomas prays for them both.

He *wills* his eyes to stop hurting, the blinders to fall away, the blurs to sharpen.

But they merge into a single, searing, frightening blindfold.

15

Thomas has waited agonizing weeks for a place on a U.S. Sanitary Commission steamer that ferries wounded and sick north for distribution to hospitals. Yet the moment his comrades deliver him to the wharf, bid farewell, he feels abandoned, as alone and frightened as when he fell into slavery.

Utterly helpless, he pays scrupulous attention as a pair of well-spoken ladies shepherd him on board. Guiding him step by step, they explain he must lie down on a quilt spread over the deck. "There's a patient already on your left." "Another will soon be on your right."

In the muggy heat, rusty, greasy smells of blood and sickness taint his every breath, and no sooner is he flat on his back then the sun rams red-hot pokers into his thickly bandaged eyes, stoking the live coals into roaring fire. Desperate for relief, he tips his head to one side, then the other. Finding none, he grinds his teeth to stop himself from adding his cries to the screams, fevered ravings, groans and moans rising above soothing shushes, the soft swish and drag of skirts, clatter of buckets, tin cups, murmured offers of milk punch, tea—

Abruptly, he realizes the arm pressing his left ends at the elbow, the leg now against his right stops at the thigh. Amputees! Their lost limbs can't be restored. But he's got his eyes, and as the engines thrum into life, he pictures the steamer carrying him out of darkness into light.

16

At Newark's General Hospital, Thomas senses consideration as well as discipline in the Night Watch's muted but firm welcome, brisk escort up two sets of stairs, past areas humming with purposeful activity to a bed near open windows through which wafts wholesome air.

As Thomas climbs in and settles, a soft mattress, crisp sheets smelling of sun and soap further support the Night Watch's boast that this hospital is "the Union's finest."

"The boys in the other beds will fill you in after they waken," the Night Watch continues, squeezing his shoulder encouragingly. "Just don't expect any pampering. Our nurses are all men, and the hospital is operated like a well run camp.

"Ambulatory patients march to meals upon sounding of the bugle. The Ward Master might let a nurse bring you yours, but you must get up for the Attending Surgeon's Morning Visit.

"Not *when* he reaches you, mind. The minute, the *very minute* you hear the Ward Master call, 'Attention,' you've got to jump out and give a smart salute.

"There's a double row of beds on each side of the ward, not one of them empty, and the Surgeon is always changing where he starts his Visit. He's also *extremely* particular. So even if you have to wait until he's examined and prescribed for everybody else, which can take a couple hours, *don't* sit on your bed or get back in. Don't even lean on it. Stay standing, and stand straight. You understand?"

Thomas, eager to prove himself worthy of care, wastes no time responding. "Yes sir."

"Good lad! You must be done in, so I'll leave you be."

Thomas is exhausted. But if his sight isn't restored, he'll have to live all the years that lie ahead trapped in darkness, at the mercy of strangers for every little thing.

So he does not sleep.

He prays.

Please, let it not be too late for the extremely particular Attending Surgeon in this fine hospital to save me.

~~~

Having heard the Attending Surgeon instruct the Ward Master, Thomas knows his eyewash is a mixture of alum and rum. So painful is its thrice daily administration that at the slosh of liquid, clink of metal forceps against pan, his heart quakes. And, as the nurse peels back each eyelid, applies a linen cloth saturated in wash to the eyeball, he'd faint were he not steeled in hope, belting his kindly sailor's bracing:

Steady, boy, steady!
You'll conquer and you'll fight again and again!

83

17

Thomas Sylvanus is the first Chinaman the hospital clerk has ever encountered, and the boy's not only filthy and womanish as the specimens depicted in illustrated magazines but as sly—else he wouldn't be using an Irish name. Nor could he have finagled himself into a white man's army, then hornswoggled a clever surgeon into believing his noxious case of conjunctivitis came from battle smoke and powder rather than a combination of an innate lack of cleanliness and cowardly hysteria.

Cleanliness forced on him, his eyes soon cleared of pus. Yet when assigned to jobs for recuperating patients, he knocked over kettles in the kitchen. Delivering trays to wards, he inched alongside walls. Ordered to move faster, he deliberately blundered into nurses, visitors, and ambulatory patients that failed to dodge him, sending all crashing. Obviously the coward was trying to avoid a return to the field by shamming blindness!

His ploy has been foiled, however. In the laundry, the colored washwomen coddle him for a pet, and with no opportunities to pretend blindness through deliberate clumsiness, his days in hospital are numbered.

~~~

At the smack-smack of the clerk's tread, Thomas's chest tightens as it used to for Baltimore's bully boys.

"You've a letter."

Me?

"You being blind and all, I'll read—"

"NO!" Leaping to his feet, Thomas shoots out a hand for what's his, swipes air as the bully unexpectedly sidesteps.

"Aw!"

Never in his life has Thomas received a letter, and determined not to lose it, he lurches for the flutter of white—

His fingers brush paper.

The bully, sniggering, swings out of reach. Heart thumping, blood racing, Thomas lunges and, heedless of hissed threats, grabs the bully's arm, wrestles the letter free.

~~~

The letter sweeps Thomas back to winter camp when, cooped inside by weather, he convinced the cousins that learning to read could be as easy and enjoyable as playing cards.

Whittling dozens of small wood squares, he painted each with a different letter of the alphabet in upper and lower case. Then, since the cousins could laboriously print their names in clumsy capitals, he said, "Look for the letters in your names."

Boisterously racing one another to be first, they assembled:

RICK

ARCHIE

GEORGI

Staying Matthew's hand as he tried adding E to GEORGI, Thomas elicited the sounds of each letter, combinations from the merry trio, and when he removed Rick's R, they screamed, "ICK!" in delight.

Archie made HICK to more laughter.

Everyone joined in the fun, and as the cousins sounded out, read words from letters they knew, Thomas taught them more. Before winter camp broke, they were devouring story papers.

They never did have patience for writing, though, and Jakob can't in English. Samuel only writes his Millie, Matthew his sister. So the letter must be from Lanky.

Even bringing the single sheet of paper within inches of his eyes and scorching it with his stare, however, Thomas can only make out a mess of blurry smudges.

~~~

Through the friendly Night Watch, Thomas obtains a magnifying glass. Then, aided by the hospital's kindly washwomen, he settles into a corner of the laundry between two lanterns turned high, studies the paper through the glass, raising and lowering it in hopes of turning smudges into letters, words.

The smudges pulse, but don't separate.

He moves the lanterns closer together, sets them directly on the paper, stares through the glass.

Still nothing!

Hovering over the smudges nearest the top of the page, he adjusts the levels for head and glass while maintaining a fixed stare. As his eyes start to tear, *xn* floats into view; and, as when learning, teaching how to read, he tries to think of a word with those letters.

In his head, the letters *xn* flip into *flux*. *Is the paper upside down?*

So he won't lose his place, he stabs the word with one finger and then, with his other hand, sets aside the glass, carefully moves the lanterns off the paper, swivels the page, replaces the lanterns, picks up the glass, and peers down. *Correct!*

Excitedly, he shifts the glass to the top of the page and snags *A*. The Union's recent narrow, hard-fought victory at Antietam pops into mind. *M* triggers Matthew.

Half-spelling, half guessing, he slowly pieces together *hair*.

Matthew's hair?!

Letter by letter, word by word, he plows on—

Finally, his eyes burned to cinders, head split asunder, he grasps the letter's gist: At the battle of Anteitam, Matthew's hair turned white down to the roots; the cousins, Samuel, and Jakob—every article of their clothing touched by a ball—came through unscathed; Lanky, weak from the flux, had a pass to fall out on the march and missed the fight.

~~~

In laborious, gigantic capitals on a penny card, Thomas encourages Lanky, himself: "BACK IN FIGHT SOON."

So distressing is Lanky's reply, "DISCHARGED. IN PHILLY," that Thomas feels cruel sending: "TRANSFER TO CONVALESCENT CAMP, ANNAPOLIS."

18

From his first day in convalescent camp, Thomas has applied himself to honing skills acquired back when he was walking a picket line at night, and after two months, he's become proficient at listening for people and animals, using these sounds, smells, all his senses for guideposts, warnings of obstacles. Now whole days pass without his once falling flat on his face or cutting a corner too close.

Since harsh glare blinds utterly and painfully, he paid a fellow to fashion a broader, deeper bill for his forage cap. Unable to identify officers from shoulder straps, he looks for the swift upward swoop of other fellows' arms to alert him to salute. On those occasions he sees distorted, double, even multiple, images where there should be one, he aims for a center point on which to focus. Then, careful not to stare rudely or squint suspiciously or uncertainly, he offers a steadfast gaze.

So capably does he mask his deficiencies that he's accused of malingering by fellows compelled to fall in line to rejoin their regiments although they're still so weak they have to lean on their rifles instead of carrying them.

He believes himself ready to return to the fight, too, and at morning roll call tells the sergeant, "Ready to report for duty, sir!"

~~~

In the camp's surgery, Thomas's eyes smart and tear shockingly from ammonia's sharp tang. He can't stop blinking at the shimmering Examining Surgeon and blunders more than once in attempting to carry out his simple instructions, barely manages not to yelp during the painful peeling back of eyelids, nevertheless firmly reiterates at its end, "Ready to report for duty, sir!"

"Not with cataracts."

Stunned, Thomas blurts, "Cataracts? I'm seventeen!"

Quickly he catches himself. "I mean nineteen, sir; nineteen!"

"Age isn't the problem," the Examining Surgeon explains, speaking slow and loud as if addressing someone elderly. "Your cataracts are from trauma, and since trauma cataracts don't cloud eyes like those from age, your eyes *look* clear though they're not. In fact, both your eyes are affected, so while the cataracts are partial, there's absolutely no question you see too poorly to perform a soldier's duties."

~~~

Fighting panic over the surgeon's indictment, Thomas shares his bitter news with Lanky:

"CATARACTS. DISCHARGE. WAITING PAPERS."

A card arrives by return mail:

"COME ROOM WITH ME."

19

For Thomas, Lanky's warm welcome softens the blow of discharge; his thoughtful guidance makes possible traversing streets treacherous from December ice and snow, memorizing Philadelphia's layout for the areas they frequent. By the New Year, Thomas is gaining confidence negotiating the maze of residences and small businesses that surround their rooming house, adept at tramping the neatly laid out squares where the city's hotels and restaurants are located.

At the employment to which his poor sight restricts him, however, he finds that unless he washes a window or shines a floor twice, he can't be sure it's clean. Then completing the task takes too long. And, repeatedly faulted for being slovenly or careless, he's failed to keep any job more than a few days, a week.

This time, dismissed after only a couple days, he drags back to their room, empties the coins in his pockets onto a small table, slumps into the closer of two chairs. Then, in slow, laborious clinks, he sorts the coins by size to determine their denominations, keeping a running tally of how much he has in addition to the three dollars he's just been paid. At the result, he shakes his head and, scooping the coins together in a dismally brief jingle-jangle, starts over.

Arriving at the same total, four dollars and eight-five cents, he's about to sigh—swallows it, stiffens his spine. Decisively, he shoves to one side the two dollars for his share of two weeks' rent, slides a half-dollar towards them for new shoes.

His fingers linger on the half-dollar. Finally, uncertain how many days will pass before he finds another job, he returns the coin to the side that must cover food, reaches behind him for yesterday's newspaper, and unlaces his shoes to pad their soles, worn thin, cover the holes.

The door clicks open. Recognizing Lanky's tread, Thomas doesn't look up but offers as cheerful a greeting as he can muster.

~~~

Returning from the print shop where he sets type, Lanky takes in the meaning of coins, shoes, newspaper in a sweeping glance.

But weeks ago his, "Thomas, I've recovered and am working steady. Let me cover our expenses," was too proudly refused for Lanky to try again, and his subsequent suggestion that Thomas apply for an invalid pension was as hotly rebutted: "I'm not an invalid any more than you!"

So Lanky plunges into a fresh approach. "Should a fellow that's lost an arm or leg receive a pension?"

"Of course," Thomas blazes, and as his hands still and a deepening flush shows he's made the hoped-for connection, Lanky drops into the chair beside him, admitting, "I've looked into what's necessary for submitting an application to the Bureau of Pensions. Besides a *Certificate of Disability for Discharge,* you'll need confirmation from our company captain that your cataracts and blindness are from a battle injury and you have a good character and habits. Also two witnesses—"

"I don't even know myself exactly how or when my eyes were damaged!"

"Anyone that can swear he saw you at the Seven Days battles will do and you've already got one witness in me. We can look for a second at one of the refreshment saloons."

When traveling from training camp to Washington, their regiment stopped at the Union Volunteer Refreshment Saloon in Southwark, and Thomas well remembers his amazement over its ladies and gentlemen performing the duties of servants to feed hungry soldiers, the volunteer server at his table refilling his coffee mug, pressing seconds and thirds on him as much as his comrades.

Now, stepping into the Union with Lanky, Thomas is engulfed in savory steamy heat, the fragrance of coffee, rumble of talk, clatter of plates and cutlery from hundreds of soldiers eating at long tables, the mouth-watering memory of cold boiled ham, strong cheese, and soft white bread with sweet butter that their regiment enjoyed.

His sight as cobwebby as the remembered tastes are sharp on his tongue, his throat lumps at all he's lost, gratitude for Lanky.

Pulling him close, Thomas hollers into his ear. "I can't pick out a single face. What about you?"

Lanky, chuckling, robs him of his cap and bellows, "Dance a jig between the tables singing *Yankee Doodle Dandy.*"

The suggestion shoots Thomas back to training camp when, together with his comrades, he jovially responded to queries of "What are you?"

Then Lanky adds, "I'll wait for you here by the door."

Feeling as abandoned as on the steamer from Harrison's Landing, Thomas sternly admonishes: *Come cheer up my boy, with one heart let us sing!* And, girded in the kindly sailor's cheer, he raises voice and legs mightily, capers down the aisle, silently praying that he won't blunder into servers, that he'll be noticed despite the saloon's commotion and a witness will respond to his piercing but still tuneful:

"Father and I went down to camp

Along with Captain Gooding

And there we saw the men and boys,

Including a Chinese Yankee."

To his relief, laughter and applause greet his advance, ripple through each row of diners. Still in uniform since he can afford no other clothing, he pretends himself in transit like the soldiers who, between verses, join in the chorus, "Yankee doodle, keep it up."

Where their hilarity increases with every roar of its final line, "And with the girls be handy," however, his energy, like his air castle, begins to sag.

By the time he prances up to the saloon's door, there's no pretending his uniform makes him a soldier, no hiding his disappointment that there's been no shout of recognition.

"We'll find someone at the Cooper Shop," Lanky encourages.

~~~

The second refreshment saloon is smaller, the noise more intense, and having already belted all thirteen verses *and* the chorus of *Yankee Doodle* multiple times, Thomas's throat hurts, his voice cracks. Moreover, the long trudge from the Union shredded the paper stuffed into his shoes, letting in grit that's rubbing raw his feet, so his jig is less lively.

Few soldiers applaud or, with the exception of the single line, "Mind the music and the step," join in the chorus.

Some hoot and sneer, "Chink!" "Where's your tail?" and there's no comrade beside him to correct, "Our Thomas is a Chinese *Yankee*."

But he labors on, reminding himself sternly his goal is not to win approval but snag attention, net a witness.

Midway through the final row of tables, there's a, "Well blow me down if it ain't Chinese Tom!"

His heart hammering, Thomas halts, turns in its direction—hears the distinctive guffaw, snide tone of a corporal in Company K.

"I forgot! It's *Blind* Tom now!"

Still unable to locate the familiar pointy face but certain no comrade or anyone else from their regiment is present or they'd have hailed him, Thomas plasters on a smile.

All at once, Lanky is beside him, saying, "You're right, Corporal. Our Thomas is blind, so he's applying for an invalid pension, and he needs two witnesses. I'm one. You can be his second."

"Can but won't," the corporal snickers.

Lanky, bending till the two are head to head, retorts, "Oh, yes, you will," in a tone that brooks no denial.

If he says something more, Thomas doesn't catch it. But a moment later, the corporal is rising, clapping him on the back.

"I was just funning. Course I'll be your witness."

20

Witness statements as well as claims to the Bureau of Pensions must be notarized, and while applicants don't have to give the agency its fee of five dollars until receipt of the first pension payment, there's no advance, so Thomas pounds the pavements seeking employment.

On streets that are new to him, he strives to make sense out of shapes and shadows, calling on the faintest scent or sound, slightest quiver in the air for clues. During interviews, he offers to demonstrate for free that his inability to soldier won't affect job performance. Given a trial, he works double-time to please. Told he falls short, he renews his search.

Weary beyond measure, he collapses into bed at night. Sleep doesn't come easily, though. Lying beside him, Lanky is as wakeful, and for the same reasons.

As pleased as they both are that the President's proclaimed those enslaved in Confederate territory to be forever free and ordered the Union Army to emancipate slaves rather than return them to their masters, the Proclamation can't be enforced in the Confederacy. Nor does it apply to states like Maryland that aren't in rebellion. So slavery hasn't really ended and won't unless the Union prevails.

But the Union suffered a terrible drubbing at Fredericksburg, the last major battle, and support for the war has been plummeting, demands to stop the bloodshed through a negotiated peace growing.

From all accounts, soldiers are deserting in droves. Alarmingly, the Confederacy might win.

Lanky has confided he feels like a deserter.

Thomas, desperate to do something to aid the fight, decides that the very next time the boom of cannon signals the imminent arrival of soldiers at the Union Refreshment Saloon, he'll respond.

~~~

To Thomas's pleasure, the servers at the Union recognize him and, warmly accepting his offer of help, send him to the kitchen.

Since entire regiments must be served in short amounts of time, the Union's demands are greater than the establishments from which he's been sacked. Its matronly supervisor is as exacting as the strictest officer at inspection. When she criticizes him for being too slow, the cabbage and onion he's chopping as coarse and uneven, he braces for dismissal.

Barking, "A worker is only as good as his tools," she takes his knife, gives it a few quick strokes on a sharpening rod, hands it back. "You'll find you can work faster now and get better results."

During clean-up, the ladies and gentlemen volunteering as servers in the saloon disappear. Everybody in the kitchen pitches in. Even the supervisor who, returning one in four of the dishes he's washed for failing to pass muster, instructs, "Always scrape off the leftover bits of food before you wash."

When he lags behind the other fellows mopping floors, the speediest advises, "Make wider arcs with your mop and you'll be twice as fast."

While washing windows, his eyes smart and water, his nose prickles from vinegar's tang. About to wipe a pane dry, a girl snatches his rag. "Don't spoil the lovely shine vinegar's given the glass." She offers him a sheet of crumpled newspaper. "Cloth leaves streaks, this won't."

These same volunteers, curious as they are helpful, ply him with questions, and since they know from his search for a battle witness that he's applying for an invalid pension, he finds himself sharing his difficulties in keeping a job.

"It's a disgrace how many disabled veterans have been reduced to begging on the streets," the supervisor rails. "Are you working now?"

"At the moment, we all are," a wag jokes.

Thomas smiles ruefully. "I don't have a job."

"You will," the supervisor assures. "The housekeeper at an elegant hotel on Chestnut Street just told me about an opening in their kitchen. I'll recommend you."

21

Hired as a general kitchen boy, Thomas puts into practice the tips he's learned from the Union's kitchen, and while he can't equal fellow workers in efficiency or proficiency, a day passes, then one week, a second, a milestone third without the dreaded words of dismissal.

Receiving steady wages, Thomas's money worries quiet. His feet float in new shoes. His fingers riffle the coins in his pockets just to hear their merry jingle.

As much as he can, he still volunteers at the Union. What he really wants is to march out of the saloon with the soldiers, though, and on the streets, the bells and whistles of troop trains call:

Come back! Come back!

Then the Bureau of Pensions denies his claim.

"Appeal the ruling," Lanky urges.

"No, I'm *not* an invalid in need of a pension, not anymore."

"You're right," Lanky concedes. "You *are* doing well. But cataracts don't go away. They get worse. So you're either as blind as at discharge or blinder. I, on the other hand, haven't suffered an attack of flux in months, and I've fully recovered my strength, so I'll be reenlisting."

"I'll go with you!"

"What doctor would mark you fit for service?"

Thomas hides his hurt in a laugh.

"One like our regimental surgeon. *He* marked me fit for the Eighty-first Pennsylvania after tapping my chest a couple times."

"Too bad your eyesight can't match your spirit," Lanky says soberly. "In the chaos of battle, you'd be a danger. Why don't you join the I.C.?"

I.C., the Invalid Corps that's forming for disabled soldiers deemed capable of garrison duty, serving as hospital guards and attendants.

I.C., what the quartermaster stamps on sides of rotten meat, moldy ammunition to indicate they've been Inspected, Condemned.

Crushed that Lanky should consider him similarly wanting, Thomas almost misses his comrade's admission, "I'm going back to our old regiment."

22

At Lanky's departure, it seems to Thomas the very radiators in the rooming house clang and wail his loneliness. Resolved to move forward, he makes a plan: Exchanging uniform for civilian garb, he'll seek enrollment as a new recruit in a new regiment.

There are none newer than those being organized for colored. He's too late for the First North Carolina Colored Volunteers, formed weeks after the Emancipation Proclamation allowed freedmen to enroll in the Union Army, but recruiters for a second, the Fifty-fourth Massachusetts Colored Volunteer Infantry, are here in Philadelphia right now, and his cataracts invisible to the naked eye, there's no reason they should refuse him.

No reason except the recruiters' surgeon is as meticulous as the one for the Eighty-first Pennsylvania was not.

His mistake: He should have gone to an existing regiment. Depleted by heavy casualties and massive desertions, their surgeons are likely more cursory in their examinations.

Except they aren't, at least not the ones he tries, who tell him, "Loss of sight in your left eye doesn't disqualify you from service. The loss of sight in your right, your musket eye, does."

Surrendering, he volunteers for the Invalid Corps.

"Yours is a hopeless case of disability," its Examining Surgeon says, "rendering you unfit for service of any kind."

No, not *any* kind.

He's proven himself sufficiently fit for one service, and at the cannon's boom, signaling the imminent arrival of a troop train, the need for volunteers at the Union to help prepare food, clean up, he races to report for duty. But his friendships in the Union's and hotel's kitchens don't go beyond their walls, and he aches for the camaraderie lost to him.

EMERGENCY
1863
June – September

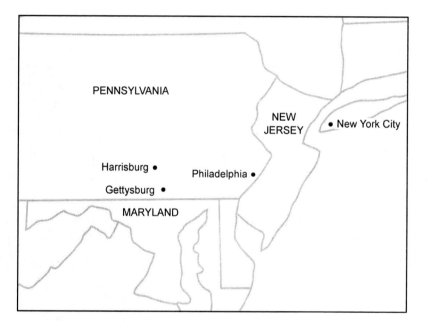

23

At newsboys' shouts that the enemy's on the march, aiming to invade Pennsylvania, Thomas all but leaps out of his skin.

To his astonishment, most people go about their business as usual. No volunteer at the Union Refreshment Saloon shares his alarm, and his fellow workers in the hotel kitchen scoff:

"The reports are just scare tactics to raise troops."

"Like the threat of invasion after Antietam."

"Hah! What a fizzle!"

"Yeah, but the army got plenty of new recruits."

"Cannon fodder, you mean."

"The same trick's not gonna work twice."

Can the threat of invasion really be a sham?

The governor must believe it true since he's authorized a Ninety-Day Emergency Militia to drive out the invaders. Civic and military leaders stand on street corners, exhorting, "Citizens, arise! Defend your state!"

Few heed their call, though, and Thomas has been too thoroughly inspected and condemned to try.

Then refugees start fleeing the state's border counties, proof positive the invasion *isn't* a sham, and as they shrill terrifying tales of rebel raiders burning, destroying property, stealing horses, cattle, and grain, deliberately going after and capturing colored, even babies in cradles, sending them south, Thomas realizes that unless the state mounts an

105

effective resistance, and soon, the Confederate Army will march right into Philadelphia!

Panicked, he considers running once more.

No!

He won't be driven out.

Or go back to slavery.

Not if he's dragged back south.

Not here in this city as costumed jape—

24

A bona fide Celestial doorman in native costume would, in the hotelier's view, distinguish his hotel as unique. But his Celestial kitchen boy refuses to cooperate!

Even threatened with firing, the ingrate won't dress in black silk pants, brocaded jacket, cloth slippers, and skull cap; or, at the very least, attach a false queue to his hair. Nor will he countenance clasping his hands and bowing low to greet guests.

Furious, the hotelier *would* fire him. Except every room is packed with guests, and now that recruiters for the Emergency Militia have started enticing the greedy and gullible with lavish bounties for enrollment, the hotel's losing workers faster than they can be replaced.

The hotelier, hands shaking, pours himself a large brandy. As though he doesn't have troubles enough, rumor has it that rebel generals—in search of a shoe factory for their barefoot men—have blundered upon the Army of the Potomac mere hours away in Gettysburg, and the skirmish has flared into battle!

He gulps down the brandy. A tad steadier, he pours another. He's been tripping over his own feet from nerves, and he has to seat his frantic guests at the windows for the governor's address from the iron grilled balcony of the swank Continental Hotel across the street—

~~~

Thomas, praying rumors of nearby battle unfounded, dashes out the kitchen door, squeezes into the noisy crush of people jamming the street for the governor's address. He discovers the governor's been delayed and a Negro, urged to climb onto the balcony to sing *The Star-Spangled Banner,* appears to be lifting both his hands to the darkening sky.

"Oh! Say, can you see…"

As the call soars to Heaven, a hush falls over the crowd, Thomas's heart swells with emotion. By "the rockets' red glare, the bombs bursting in air," he's marching alongside his comrades; the regiment's color sergeant, holding aloft the flag of the stars, is boldly leading the way into the fight at Gettysburg—

Elbows stab, shoulders knock, jolting Thomas back into the crowded street. The Negro singer is receding into the shadows, and people, buzzing the governor has arrived, are pushing, shoving closer to the balcony on which a silhouette's emerging from a blaze of light.

The governor plunges directly into harried confirmation that the Confederate and Union armies are locked in battle at Gettysburg. Gloomily, he reveals the day's bloody contest has ended inconclusively. Come morning, the two armies will take up arms again, and in the name of duty and of manhood, he exhorts earnestly for every man who loves liberty to enlist.

Listening, Thomas' mind flashes on the dozens of regiments raised the last few weeks. Not only have they failed to halt the enemy's advance, but sending ill equipped, untrained thousands to the front has caused boundless confusion.

How can more militia help?

Won't raw recruits be whipped to pieces?

All around him people are echoing the governor's appeal for enrollments. There's the distinctive beat of recruiters' drums.

Thomas pushes through the crowd, shouting, "I'm a seasoned soldier. Take me."

"I'll go, too," rasps a voice he recognizes as belonging to Frank, the burly coal delivery man.

25

Even if he weren't twice Thomas's girth and age, Frank would've ignored the multiple calls for volunteers these past two years, and since he says what he thinks, everybody in his neighborhood and on his delivery route knows why: The greedy masters and meddlesome do-gooders responsible for this war can bloody well fight it themselves!

But any man worth his salt defends his home against invasion. So given the Union Army's frighteningly narrow victory at Gettysburg while the Fifty-first Regiment is enrolling, Frank musters in alongside Thomas and applies his old-dog self to learning new tricks at training camp lest the invaders mount another attack.

Following barked instructions for loading and firing a musket is harder than Frank expected. Truth to tell, only Thomas's hand-over-hand guidance saves him from shooting off a thumb or foot. Other fellows keep dropping their weapons when presenting arms, turning left though ordered to face right.

At the news the invaders have turned tail and are slinking back to Dixie dragging a wagon train of wounded stretching seventeen miles, everybody cheers. Widower and childless though he be, Frank would like nothing better than to quit and go home himself. Having given his oath to serve ninety-days, however, he's honor bound to stick out training camp in Harrisburg, entrain for provost and clean-up duty in Gettysburg.

His shoulder jolting against Frank's on the train, Thomas thinks of his comrades in the Eighty-first Pennsylvania. To keep them alive, he's avoided anyone reading casualty lists out loud. But he can't stop fretting over how they are. Nor can he quell his rising hope that he can and will return to them. These past weeks in training camp, he's not only shown he's capable of drilling, loading and firing a musket, but helped others learn, and if he's as successful performing the duties of a soldier in the field....

As the train steams into Gettysburg, such awful miasmas gust in the carriage windows, Frank can scarce breathe. At the depot, stacks of closed coffins await loading, and marching through town, every building they pass seems to be missing bricks, scarred by bullets, embedded with shells.

A prior regiment has already collected thousands of muskets, bayonets, rounds of small-arms ammunition, knapsacks, and blankets dropped in the heat of the fight. Yet the trampled, blood-soaked fields remain littered with weapons, equipment, broken caissons and wagons that must be gathered.

To keep out scavengers, souvenir hunters, and curiosity seekers, the Fifty-first has to check passes. As provosts enforcing martial law, they stand guard, walk patrols. Their duties aren't taxing. But whether in field or town or at an entrance to the rows upon rows of hospital wall tents, there's no escaping the screams of the wounded. Even during sleep, Frank is wakened by their cries, Thomas's groaning, twitching torments. Nor are the dead any less restless: Nights, the greenish phosphorescence of unhappy spirits hover above acres and acres of graves; daylight makes visible hands and feet which poke from the soil, scrabbling to get out, pleading to be among those found and claimed by relatives for exhumation, embalming, coffining, a final journey home.

Truth to tell, Frank can't distinguish between the stink of their rot and the dead horses—grossly bloated and giving off foul gasses—still being dragged one by one into heaps by mule teams for disposal. These carcasses, doused with coal oil, are torched, and so bad is the stench of smoldering burning flesh that frequent whiffs of peppermint oil don't always succeed in stopping his stomach from revolting. He finds the chloride of lime spread to combat pestilence almost as offensive.

Like everyone for miles around, he's red-eyed and weepy from the irritating smoke. Thomas, his poor eyes swollen into slits, can't see beans. But his inability to read passes presented to him when standing guard isn't any different from those who don't know their letters. Despite his wincingly slow prying open of eyelids encrusted in the night, he's always first at morning roll call. He holds his own in any detail.

That's certainly more than can be said for the warmongers at whose door the boy's ruined eyes and this stinking mess should be laid. Fact is, the bloodshed could've ended back when recruiters on both sides, offering ever larger bounties, failed to drum up enough volunteers to keep the fight going. And the war *would* be over except the powerful—again, on both sides—pushed for, and got, Conscription Acts *forcing* men to fight. Not their own sons, of course. *They* have the option of paying a commutation fee to their government or willy-nilly getting a substitute to fight in their place!

SUBSTITUTE
1863
August - October

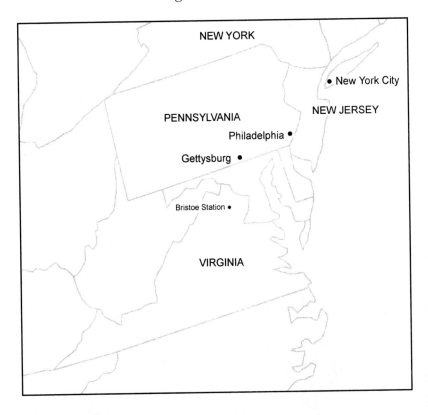

NEW YORK

• New York City

NEW JERSEY

PENNSYLVANIA

Philadelphia •

Gettysburg •

Bristoe Station •

VIRGINIA

26

Thomas accepts the Conscription Act as he does martial law in Gettysburg: a temporary necessity borne of emergency. What he can't accept is others risking injury and death to secure *his* freedom, especially not now he's proved he *can* perform a soldier's duties, albeit not all, nor well enough to convince his old regiment to let him back. With luck, the Conscription Act could give him the means to return to the fight.

Talk is that substitutes don't undergo medical examinations, and littering the camp are broadsides screaming:

WANTED! WANTED!
SUBSTITUTES
MILITARY AND NAVAL
CASH RIGHT DOWN!

The unreadable smudges below must be instructions for how to apply, where to go. But when Thomas hands the broadside to Frank, he crumples it in disgust, snorting, "This is blood money!"

"I don't want a red cent!" Thomas protests. "Just to get back into the Army of the Potomac and finish the fight."

~~~

Unable to convince Thomas of his wrong-headedness, Frank hopes to at least save the boy from scoundrel brokers and agents who

115

are reeling in the gullible with wild offers of cash. Making in-person evaluations after they get back to Philly would be safest. Fearful of recognition as a disabled veteran, however, Thomas is insisting on going to New York, catching the first available train after muster-out. So Frank scours advertisements in newspapers for those placed by principals rather than brokers and agents, reading them out loud to Thomas.

Examining them together for sincerity, they jointly settle on:

"Good family man has square deal for
man willing to serve as substitute.
Apply G.H.D., Station G, New York."

~~~

One person—a Thomas Sylvanus—responds to his advertisement, and George Dearborn, studying the penciled scrawl, seesaws between relief and suspicion.

He'd borrowed heavily to buy his umbrella store, and even though, thank the good Lord, his business was spared damage in July's murderous rioting over the draft, the days of lost sales cost him dear. So he hasn't any cash to spare, not a penny, and however much he further borrows, it won't come near the enormous amounts promised in other advertisements. Yet this Thomas Sylvanus replied, and without inquiring how many dollars he'll receive. *Why? Is he hiding something? Will the Board of Enrollment accept him?*

27

The commissioner for the Board of Enrollment can't step out onto the street without hearing New York City's most popular riddle, and every time he cringes anew at its pithy truth:

"How does Abe, with his Conscription Act, differ from the butchers that drive bullocks to the slaughter house?"

"Butchers drive the fat of the land to slaughter. Abe drives none but the poor."

His commitment to Union victory is unwavering, however, and too many draftees are failing to report for duty. Moreover, women and children are driving away officers sent to fetch their husbands, sons, and fathers by hurling hot water and stones!

So, trembling for his soul and the Union's, the commissioner overlooks disturbing reports of substitute brokers scouring slums and docks, coercing, outright kidnapping the poor and vulnerable for moneyed draftees to present at hearings. His head and heart heavy as the September heat, his stomach sour, he doesn't speak to his two colleagues on the Board about the despicable trade in human flesh that Conscription has spawned or the morality of forcing men to fight against their will. Instead, he restricts himself to arguing with the provost marshal, seated on his left, and the surgeon, on his right, that their criteria for accepting a substitute should be more than the mere possession of teeth for tearing open cartridges.

Nevertheless, the commissioner fails.

Taking another completed *Substitute Volunteer Enrollment* form from the stack on the bench before him, the commissioner catches the words "born in the Empire of China," launches into a blunter, more emphatic attempt to convince.

"Can't you see substitute brokers are selling the most deplorable specimens to draftees? Every single one we've approved this past week has been an ignorant foreigner, imbecile, or drunk!"

He throws the form onto the bench, thumps it with his fist. "If we continue to accept them, we risk losing the war!"

"Plenty of the men already serving are ignorant, foreign, drunks, imbeciles, and worse," the surgeon retorts.

"Gentlemen!" the provost marshal intercedes sharply. "We've a quota of 2,000 men to meet and no more time to waste."

He nods at the clerk. "Next."

Determined to hold firm, the commissioner reminds, "The War Department specifically forbids colored as substitutes and Chinese—"

But the clerk is already throwing open the door to the anteroom crammed with draftees and substitutes waiting their turn, calling above the blast of talk for the Chinaman and umbrella merchant named on the form: Thomas Sylvanus; George H. Dearborn.

~~~

George has been hanging out the anteroom's window, at first to flee its suffocating fug of sweat and cheap tobacco, then because he's riveted by the raucous ragamuffins in the street who're gathering manure, selling matches, digging through rubbish heaps, tussling over rotting morsels with yip-yapping, snarling dogs, each other.

In these children, George sees what would happen to his own

bright-eyed, well-dressed, well-fed darlings were his income reduced to a soldier's thirteen dollars a month or, Heaven forefend, he be injured, killed. Surely, then, he's right to stay at the helm of his umbrella store, pay a man to fight in his place.

Only his substitute has turned out to be a child, too, a hapless China boy in the clutches of a hefty weasel, and there's nothing that can be done about it, not now the boy's responded to the clerk's call—

⁓

To Thomas's relief, his eyes are much less puffy and tender since leaving Gettysburg, but his vision remains fuzzy, and peering at what seems to be three judges looming behind a bench, he quails: Among the documents he had to submit was a sworn statement that he's never been discharged from military service for a disability.

Will I be jailed if they catch my lie?

Tamping down his turmoil, Thomas assumes a confident stance and crosses the room in strides that are the very opposite of the hand-wringing merchant whose hurried, mincing footfalls barely keep him alongside.

The judge at the far left of the bench stands, barks, "Over here!"

Thomas, obeying, has his chin seized, lips pried apart like a slave under consideration for purchase.

Balling his hands into fists, he squelches the impulse to bite. The merchant gasps and splutters as if *he* were being examined.

"The boy's fit."

At this pronouncement, Thomas is released.

The judge at the other end of the bench rattles off something about freely swearing to three years of true and faithful service, slaps a sheet of paper on the bench, and commands, "Sign," while proffering a pen.

Thomas, still reeling from shock, stumbles forward, grasps the

119

pen, and looks down. The paper is a sea of jumbled print and, having signed the many forms with Frank's guidance, there's no possibility of hiding behind a claim of illiteracy.

Dipping the pen into the inkwell, Thomas resists the urge to pick up the paper, bring it close. *I've been declared fit! I am fit. I just have to sign.* Carefully he bends only as much as he did when fully sighted, poises the pen over the paper, willing calm.

Beneath the nib, the quivering black bits of type settle, separate, leaving a blank space suitable for a signature. He aims for it, scratches *Thomas Sylvanus.*

28

When planning his return to the fight as a substitute, Thomas understood he'd be busting into a regiment short of men because comrades had been lost to injury or death, and the survivors—having tented and fought together for over two years—would be tight-knit, resentful of replacements, particularly fellows coming late into the war for cash. But he's being marched to the Forty-second New York Infantry's camp between double rows of bayonets like a common criminal!

Too choked with humiliation to whistle a tune from his kindly sailor for comfort, yet determined to present a cheerful face, he forces out bird chirps, trembling warbles.

~~~

In the twenty-seven months since he celebrated the formation of the Forty-second New York by buying cigars from one of the Chinese peddlers outside City Hall Park, the lieutenant's not seen a Chinaman. Cannonading, shelling, and musketry have made birds almost as scarce. Yet here's a tawny complexion amidst faces fried beet-and liver-red by the angry southern sun, joyful bird calls rising above surly curses, grumbles.

According to the guards, the slipperiest scoundrels did the quick-step skedaddle between New York and Bristoe Station. The lieutenant warns the rest that henceforth, any runaways will be hunted down, their heads shaved and painted with *D*, their ankles shackled to heavy balls and chains except during drill.

By nightfall, he's twice ordered this punishment, and it's soon obvious that among these drunks, rowdies, cardsharps, and thieves, few will become effective soldiers. No wonder the War Department is pressing seasoned soldiers in three-year regiments like the Forty-second New York to reenlist for the duration of the war, promising thirty-day leaves back home on signing, plus veteran bounties of four hundred dollars. With over half the regiments in the field due to expire next year and recruits, conscripts, and substitutes like this lot, disaster looms!

China Tom, capable of loading and firing three times a minute like a veteran, is a shining exception. Studying him, the lieutenant considers:

Too young for one of the three-month regiments at the start of the war.

Not a later nine-month regiment or he'd have returned to service with a veteran's bounty, chevrons of red and blue braid on his left sleeve rather than as substitute scum.

Perhaps a stint in the state militia?

Quizzed, China Tom colors to the tips of his ears as if accused of a crime, gushes he learned how to march and shoot from an older brother, since killed, who served in another New York outfit.

"Nonsense!" the lieutenant snaps.

"Oh, not nonsense, sir," China Tom comes back, "Not from me, sir," and he snaps a smart salute, bursts into song:

"I'm a Yankee black of hair,

A true blue Chinese Yankee,

My hand is strong, my heart is warm,

122

The Union can count on me, sir!"

Listening, the lieutenant flashes to his own earnest declarations at the start of the war, heats uncomfortably. The clarity and enthusiasm he'd enjoyed then couldn't be sustained in war's reality, and neither appeals to his patriotism nor any amount of greenbacks will persuade him to reenlist. In fact, he's already resigned his commission, and the minute he receives word of its acceptance, he'll head home.

As for China Tom, his claims of reliability may be as false as his cockamamie story about a soldier-brother. Only in battle is a soldier's true colors revealed.

~~~

The lieutenant's suspicious quizzing is unnerving, and Thomas finds the constant need to peer while pretending perfect sight a strain, the persistent hostility of his fellows wounding.

To console himself, he builds air castles of the Eighty-first Pennsylvania being in the same division, stumbling upon—

No! I came back to fight, and the Forty-second New York is my regiment now.

Committing himself to winning new comrades, he parries harsh teasing and cruel jokes with jolly laughs. Assigned the filthiest, most taxing tasks, he performs them while whistling.

Still only the regiment's mules offer him acceptance, and feeding them treats, caressing their muzzles, burying his face in their manes, he's comforted by their happy nickering.

COLORS
1864
March – July
OVERLAND CAMPAIGN

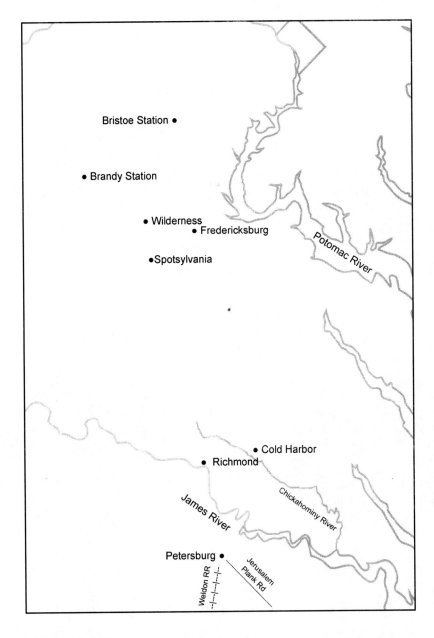

29

Silas, the Forty-second New York's mule driver, reckons China-men's slit eyes is what make them bob-bob their noggins this-away-and-that same as mules with blinkers, why the regiment's China boy, struck by a dirt-filled sock while yet a greenhorn, twisted, turned, and dipped till, chancing on the sock, he swooped down on it, lobbed it back.

'Course, it fell wide of the mark. But he threw out a challenge anyways: "Fire away, this Yankee's not afraid."

At the time, Silas don't mind admitting, he reckoned China Tom a fool, and too many of them around already, top of the list being the generals what was ordering the whole bloody army to go after the Johnnies, never mind winter coming on, roads slippery as glass from heavy rain, potholes of gooey red and yellow clay.

'Course, teams dragging canon and wagons protested in high-pitched whinnies, pitiful drawn-out brays. Many a horse and mule refused to budge 'spite of the lash, some 'cause they couldn't move no way, not with their legs plunging to their fetlocks, wheels sinking to axles. And with teams floundering, upending canon and wagons, columns of men busted in growling, cussing disorder.

Officers on horseback trotted past gaps in the line, spurs jingling, sabers rattling, hurling huge splatters of mud, bellowing: "Close up, men!" "Close up!" Gaps in the line stretched and stretched anyways, and deadbeats took advantage, falling back more and more till they done disappeared in the six days and nights of wet, ice-cold misery 'fore that doomed Mine Run campaign shivered to a bone-chilling close.

China Tom was among those falling back, but not to straggle. His breath steaming, he helped push and heave the Forty-second's wagon out of ever bigger, deeper swamp holes, sparing the scarified mules from sinking further. He dragooned more fellas into putting their shoulders to the wheel, keeping the regiment's wagon inching along.

And that ain't all.

In a hard skirmish at Robertson's Tavern, a ball split the crown of his cap in two. Flicking his head as at a fly, he stayed upright to shoot like boys done early in the war, not how veterans learned they gotta: dropping onto their bellies and digging trenches else they'd be in hospital, discharged for disability, or six feet under.

He done learned, though, and after that campaign, there ain't no mistaking China Tom be whip-smart as well as stout-hearted.

Looking back to the git-go, he always did pitch into the dirtiest chores and was respectful to old soldiers, ready with a cheery, "Howdy-doo," tender words, caresses, tasty treats for the mules.

Jumping forward to now, there ain't no complaining from nobody over his promotion to corporal.

~~~

Thomas cherishes his promotion as confirmation that despite his failure to win longed-for camaraderie, he's earned respect, and at every "Corporal Tom," his heart makes a little prideful leap. When a photographer comes to camp, he even poses for a carte de visite.

The photographic card is only about two inches by three, far too small for him to identify himself. But alone and under good light, he examines his image closely through a magnifying glass, and his heart

128

lifts: Although his sight is as ravaged as the national flag he's holding, his eyes look as faultless as his borrowed regulation cap.

Memory niggles like a worm in an apple, spoiling his pleasure.

During the skirmish at Robertson's Tavern, he couldn't distinguish between gray and faded blue. So he only dared shoot into the flash of musket fire, and after a ball split his cap in two, glare would have blinded him completely were it not for heavily clouded skies.

Ever since, he's pocketed a second cap in reserve. Grilling veterans of last year's battles, he's also gleaned pointers for fights to come. But with storms swirling, snowdrifts banking high, freezing in sleety rain, the Army of the Potomac's been burrowed in winter quarters at Brandy Station, so he's yet to be truly tested.

30

To Thomas's dismay, northern generals have, like southern masters, gone far beyond whipping and shackling runaways: Escaped slaves have been strung up wherever caught, left hanging as warnings; regiments, entire brigades have been forced to witness the execution of deserters by firing squad.

Charged with training a new group of replacements, he addresses them bluntly: "Like it or not, you're in the fight. Try running, and you'll be chased down, shot. Your best chance of getting through alive is to become the best possible soldier. That means knuckling under discipline, paying close attention, and submitting to drill, drill, and more drill."

~~~

Tiny wishes he were brave enough to run. Bullies have plagued him all his life for being a runt, and the regiment's old soldiers, touted as heroes, likewise delight in tormenting replacements, him most of all.

Just thinking about the old soldiers' favorite ploy—seizing him by the neck and then, guffawing to beat the band, hurling him, shrieking, onto a blanket pulled taut, tossing him higher and higher—makes him break out in a cold sweat, his stomach wobble, and he hurriedly claps his hands over his mouth, gulps sour bile, invokes Corporal Tom's ditty for bolstering courage:

Come cheer up, my boy,
'Tis to honor you're called,
Steady, boy, steady!
You'll fight and you'll conquer—

Rough hands grip his scruff, yank Tiny off his feet.

Belting, *Steady, boy, steady,* he bites his lips, sealing in the screams and sobs that leap into his throat. Released to a bone-jarring landing, his teeth sink into his lips, and he tastes blood, but not a whimper leaks. Then the blanket cracks and snaps sickeningly, shooting him in the air, and his eyes, pants flood in hot wet shame....

~~~

Soaked in sweaty panic, Thomas realizes, *I can't overcome my limitations any more than Tiny.*

When putting his squad of replacements through their paces, they blur together no matter how hard he blinks or stares. His hearing catches missteps, but he often can't identify who is at fault. *How many noiseless, possibly critical mistakes, am I missing?*

31

In regimental drills, Thomas's squad performs so well they don't just garner praise from their company captain but the colonel.

Even so, with spring heralding a new season of fighting, Lanky's "In the chaos of battle, you'd be a danger," swells louder, more insistent, as does the Confederacy's troubling threat that captured colored soldiers will be treated as slaves, alarming reports of Johnnies shooting unarmed colored prisoners in the field, making him jittery as Tiny.

~~~

Heeding Corporal Tom's instructions to their squad, Tiny is wearing his lighter sack coat for the Army of the Potomac's march from their winter quarters, carrying nothing in the way of baggage save an extra shirt, pair of socks, a half tent, and two blankets, one wool, the other gum. Yet he's sweating and panting as much as on their mock march when, ignoring the corporal's, "Pack light," they all stuffed their knapsacks and, in less than an hour under their leaden loads, were dripping and wheezing for breath with every grinding, chafing footfall.

Nor can he shed what's got him lathered—his belief he'll soon be as shattered and bloodied as the regiment's shell-torn, bullet-riddled colors....

At the order to halt and make camp outside the blood-soaked, devil-woods of the Wilderness, Silas fumes. His mules got bigger brains than the generals!

Come nightfall, no mule or horse can settle. 'Spite of campfires lit, the skin of every fella's gotta be creeping and crawling like his. Not a voice is raised in song, not even whistling Corporal Tom's. Then moonrise rouses yester year's dead, pricking old soldiers into recollecting how them scrub oak and pines—cramped thick and close and entangled in spiky vines—done shut out sun and crumbled battle lines, forcing them to fight in small groups or on their own hook. How, shooting at enemy what couldn't be seen, their rifle blasts sparked tinder-dry brush and they feared an evil wind would lick them sparks into flame....

With every word, slack-jawed greenhorn replacements turn greener 'cause even unsalted in battle, they grasp what them fool generals ain't: The army gonna be in that same mess on the morrow.

~~~

His squad fairly rattling from nerves, Thomas steels his own and, praying moonlight lends convincing gravity to his eighteen years, assures: "Once the fighting starts, everything except staying alive will fall away, your hands and feet will automatically do what you've learned in drill."

~~~

In the murky wood's stifling smoke and deadly roar, his terror of losing Corporal Tom outstrips all else, and Tiny thrashes and crawls at

133

the tail end of his squad in a mad panic of ragged, choked breaths, heedless of musket balls whining perilously near, sharp slaps of branches, thorns snagging and ripping clothes, slicing skin. He stands, kneels, or lies as they do to shoot, clumsily tearing open a cartridge with his teeth in a burst of bitter grit. His trembling fingers slip-slide it into the blistering hot gun barrel, snatch hold of the ramrod, shove paper down for wadding, cock the hammer, fumble for a percussion cap from the pouch, stick it onto the cone, jerk the rifle to his shoulder. His eyes squeeze shut, he braces for the blast, fires. At the kick to his shoulder, he reaches for another cartridge—

~~~

Fast as stretcher bearers set down their screaming, groaning burdens in the blood-soaked dirt front of the surgeons' tents, Silas grabs cartridge boxes from the wagon for them to tote back into the devil-woods' smoky clang.

Smoke got every bearer squinting and bob-bobbing their noggins like Corporal Tom. Not just them neither but the walking-wounded lurching out like headless chickens, dragging shattered limbs, clutching spilled guts; the provosts demanding, "Show blood," driving back fellas what can't, never mind they be supporting comrades, keeping them from collapsing.

Then a wind kick up, the dread smell of burning and stinging cinders gust out, and there be the awful pop-pop-pop of cartridge boxes exploding like strings of fire crackers, high-pitched shrieks—

~~~

The drums beating withdrawal long silent, Thomas's eyes and heart still howl at the unspeakable horrors of the Wilderness. His blood races from its dreadful excitement, the thrill that he *and* his squad proved equal to their duties, came through with nothing more than superficial burns, scratches.

Tramping to the next fight, he chants the praise song of a colored regiment:

Jesus make de blind to see,
Jesus make de cripple walk,
Jesus make de deaf to hear.
Walk in, kind Jesus,
No man can hinder me....

32

Even more scared now he's experienced battle's terrors, Tiny's desperate for home, and he could easily get there by slipping into the masses of walking wounded boarding steamers at river landings.

But loyalty to Corporal Tom keeps him staggering on the heels of his squad in swelteringly hot, dusty marches; splashing across rivers on unstable pontoon bridges; trembling in line of battle; sobbing huzzahs while charging with fixed bayonet into mad rat-a-tats of rifles, hissing shot....

~~~

Thomas's eyes sizzle, threatening to burst like overripe boils. Try as he might, he sometimes can't make out more than fluttery shadows.

Blanketed in battle smoke, though, he's at no greater disadvantage during fights than soldiers boasting perfect vision, and almost every day, rain falls like a blessing, often more than once, soothing his eyes, dissolving the shadows....

~~~

Rain having pelted down in torrents since afternoon, the wind raw and sharp, Tiny's soaked, chilled to the bone, and his teeth clatter uncontrollably as his shoes squelch through mud into position for another assault. But he doesn't mind a whit. So dark is the night that each fellow is under orders to clasp the shoulder directly in front of his own for guidance, and for as long as nothing's visible, the dread command, "Forward" won't come.

~~~

Silas ain't spitting tobacco juice so much as disgust: Since night, rain, and thick fog eased into morning mist, Union generals safe in headquarters near the Spotsylvania Court House have sent countless regiments of stout-hearted boys roaring 'cross a ravine soft and muddy as the slurry sucking at his boots, then slogging up a steep rise, clawing over spiked saplings to get to the enemy breastworks.

True, the Rebs ain't got no canon mowing the boys down, and from where he be studying their breastworks through a found spyglass, crazed specks of blue and gray be popping up from clouds of smoke, dropping back down; colors be swaying, plunging as their bearers fall, rearing up again if others manage to seize the flagstaff—

~~~

In the hellfire of flaming guns and eye-watering, choking smoke, screaming wounded, Thomas hurls himself, his squad into a rally round the Forty-second's colors that swiftly plummets into desperate defense.

Swallowed up in a fearful thwock of balls puncturing flesh, shattering bone, awful howls and shrieks, the blistering sting of a ball sears his neck, silk sweeps across his cheek. Instinctively, he grabs—snatches a tattered length of silk, another, grappling folds stiff from blood amidst the fierce heat and racket of musketry until fingers clutch flagstaff sticky with gore and gristle.

137

At its weight, unwieldy length, he totters—and the colors slip.
No!

Tightening his grip on the flagstaff, he struggles to raise the proud colors in spite of the knocking and jostling from the bedlam raging around him, the whine and sting of balls—at last succeeds. But not for long unless he finds a foothold.

Warily, he prods and pokes a foot into the bodies heaped around him.

One foot anchored, he seeks a place to lodge his other.

Finally, both feet firmly planted, he likewise wedges the flagstaff, roars into song for his squad, their regiment, himself:

"Forty-second, fire away!

New Yorkers aren't afraid, sir!

Yankee Doodle! Fire away!

The Union can count on us, sir!"

33

Days after driving the rebels from their breastworks, the regiment's newly appointed color sergeant's head yet spins from the horror of losing every member of the color guard, the wonder of China Tom seizing and hoisting aloft the Forty-second New York's flag as the last man fell.

With China Tom's heroic catch and the colors flying, every man jack in the regiment gave his all to the fight: shooting, bayoneting Johnnies in face and chest, jumping on top of the bloodied breastworks to fire, slipping on the gore, then—if not picked off—sliding, leaping down to reload and hopping up again, often over the bodies of fellows lying where they dropped, trampling them into the mud.

Not only that! Till the butchery ended, China Tom gave the Johnnies fits by singing, and as the multiple holes in his sleeves, pants, scorch marks on his face and neck testify, balls flying thick and mean as hornets zinged close enough to sear and sting.

He can't possibly be scared that color guards are the special target of sharp shooters, so why in tarnation is he stuttering and stammering about getting chosen!

~~~

To be chosen for the color guard is an honor Thomas has never dared hope for, not even when posing for the carte de visite, and can't

accept. Not when the fireballs in his head are scorching shadow images into ash. But admitting the seriousness of his defect would mean
dismissal.

Sarge snorts impatiently. "Come on, lad."

"I, my—"

"Lands sakes, spit it out!"

"My eyes are bad. I—"

"I can bloody well see they're swollen red and oozy," Sarge snaps.
"I've got the shakes and rheumatics to boot. We're also neither of
us near the height of our previous color bearers. Top of that, I warrant we've not got their strength. Tell you what, though. We're here.
They're not. So we've got to make do. Ben and I will be in the lead
carrying the flags. You'll be in the rear."

Thomas, searching for a response, senses Sarge's right side shifting—*arm rising to salute an officer?*—half lifts his own, feels rough
canvas thrust into his hand.

"Here's my flag carrier to tie around your waist in case you've got
to pick up the colors again. I can manage without."

34

Tiny has borne a nerve-racking month of panicky, brutal fights and grueling marches by repeating, *I got through Spotsylvania; no battle can be bloodier.* But anyone with eyes can see the Army of the Potomac doesn't stand a chance against the formidable batteries spiking the rebel earthworks here in Cold Harbor.

Hoping that at least his body can go home, Tiny borrows a stubby pencil, begs a scrap of paper on which to write his name and address from one of the many soldiers similarly occupied. He's careful to press the pencil point hard so his mother won't be troubled by shaky lettering.

As he starts pinning the scrap to his coat, he's struck by its similarity to the white circle affixed on a condemned deserter's chest for a target—stabs a finger. Blood beads, smears the paper, and Tiny, thrusting it into a pocket for the burial detail to find, throws himself into a rowdy game of cards with his squad.

But nothing—not their forced laughter or his own, nor ever wilder wagering—blocks his memories of the execution that their division was forced to witness, the fact that charging the rebel batteries tomorrow, he'll be as much of a mark and as frightened as the deserter openly sobbing in front of the firing squad.

As dead, too, despite Corporal Tom's training.

Thomas is grateful for the flag carrier tied around his waist. Having lost both his extra deep brimmed caps, however, strong glare blinds no matter how low he tugs a regular cap over his eyes, forcing him to study the ground, follow the rise and fall of what must be legs, shoes—until suffocating dust clamps his eyelids shut, obscuring all.

His daily prayer is for restorative showers, dull skies, and he reviews the order in which the color guard marches as frequently and fervently as the chaplain clicks his rosary beads:

In the lead, providing direction for the regiment, are Sarge with the Forty-second's blue silk; Ben the Stars and Stripes.

Josh marches between them, ready to swoop up the colors should Sarge fall.

Dutch and Zeke cover Ben and Josh.

Jake marches behind Sarge.

Alongside, in the line of file closers, go Andy and Sam.

I'm last.

So chances are I won't have to pick up the colors.

Or, by staying hard on the heels of Andy and Sam, I'll be able to feel the colors fall, as I did before, then seize the flagstaff, secure it in the carrier, and step shoulder to shoulder with whoever is holding the other flag for guidance.

Unless there is no one—

~~~

Standing in line of battle for the assault against the rebel earthworks, Sarge roils in the tempest of love, longing, and dread that precedes every fight, a tingling chill which isn't from the dense pre-dawn fog but his malaria acting up.

There's no question of falling out. Were he and all the other soldiers with maladies to do so, the regiment would be devastated, and he prays the shakes won't strike until the doomed charge is over, that he'll live to go home when the Forty-second New York's three years are up nineteen days hence—but only if he still possesses a pair of arms to embrace his wife, swing his son high, legs to walk his copper's beat.

Shivering, he wonders whether he has time to get his flag carrier back from China Tom: The rebel guns directly ahead are quiet, but elsewhere the miles of earthworks are rumbling, giving rise to alarming shrieks and yells—

"Get ready, men!" the colonel barks.

Clenching his jaws against his shakes, Sarge hefts the long flagstaff for the regiment's colors off the ground onto his right hip. Then, firming his grip with his left hand, he slides his right to shoulder height as smoothly as the shakes and his joints, creaking from rheumatics, permit; rests his elbow against the staff, steadying; glances up: The regiment and national colors are level.

"Forward!"

Sarge springs into the dank fog with a hurrah brave and bright as the colors, the division's brassy bugle calls, rousing a thunderous chorus from the regiment, and his blood pulses to their roar, the beat from drums, horses' hooves, thousands of brogans striking ground—

Rain having tamped down the plain's powdery soil during the night, there's no strangling dust. But the damp aggravates his aching joints, chills, and when a gigantic crash of artillery obliterates the crackle of skirmishers' fire ahead, his chest tightens. Stooping as if breasting a tempest, he pushes deeper into the clammy fog and metallic smoke, closer to the enemy's death-dealing, maiming guns.

~~~

One minute, Thomas is keeping pace despite the fog, shells screeching overhead, earth jumping beneath his feet.

The next, he's floundering in rolling clouds of smoke, a staggering confusion of troops, maelstrom of conflicting drum calls, shouted orders, and angry curses, a galling blizzard of hot lead that turns their brigade's charge into a bloody repulse.

In the uproar, a shrill, "Corporal T—," breaks into a wrenching howl.

Tiny!

Reaching out, Thomas is knocked flat amidst grunts of labored breath, the clatter and scrape of bayonets, knives, cups, plates, and shifting earth.

Men must be digging a trench for protection!

Wordlessly, he rolls onto his belly to add his muscle. Something sharp pierces his leg below the knee. Scrunching from it, he grits his teeth against the stabbing, plunges both hands into the dirt, claws surface clods, scoops up the soft earth beneath.

Overhead deadly shells whistle and explode, pieces thud to the ground.

Bugles and drums sound the command to rally.

"Men of New York, stand by me!"

Thomas arches up—is cuffed back down.

Scrabbling to his knees, he shouts, "That's the colonel."

"You'll be killed for nothing," a voice he doesn't recognize warns.

"I—"

"Didn't you see? We were marching into a swamp."

35

Squeezed inside the swampy cabin of the steamer ferrying survivors across the James River, Thomas's head pounds from ten nightmare days pinned under deafening, murderous bombardment; his belly rolls queasily at every dip and rise.

He's heartsick over the enormous casualties, especially the loss of Tiny, every one of the replacements he trained, all the newly appointed color guard except Sarge, Jake, and himself, but, oh, so thankful that although rebel cannonading smashed the entire Yankee assault past mending, the Army of the Potomac wasn't destroyed and, having finally given the enemy the slip under cover of darkness, can fight on.

Can I?

Bile shoots into Thomas's parched throat: If a color bearer falls now, nay, *when* a color bearer next falls, *he* will have to pick up the flag, and not only are his eyes ruined, the cut on his leg is turning poisonously hot and sore....

Defiantly, he swallows hard, tugs loose his canteen's stopper with fingers sorely battered from digging, drains its foul-tasting dregs, sings, "Yes, we'll rally 'round the flag, boys—"

Voices from every corner of the cabin chime in, vowing:

"We'll rally 'round once again,

Shouting the battle cry of Freedom!"

~~~

The sole freedom Sarge is aiming for will come when his oath of service expires in seven days and he'll no longer be duty-bound to obey generals with incorrect maps and foolhardy plans.

That's why he refused last winter's wily offer of thirty days home in exchange for reenlisting, and there've been too many unnecessary casualties, broken promises for him to accept a day's delay in going home to his wife and son, let alone some blamed higher-up's decision to postpone his muster-out for a month!

~~~

Thomas hasn't forgotten the oft-repeated promise of officers back in his first campaign, "Just another fight or two and we'll be in Richmond," and, now, dragging into musket-range of Petersburg, the final hurdle on the road to the rebel capital, he prays the Army of the Potomac will at last succeed.

Night has fallen. But he can plainly hear muffled pops of gunfire; closer, the ruckus of heavy wheels, joyful clapping and laughter, reluctant scuffing and shuffling.

Puzzled, he cranes his neck for a closer look—can't open his grit-and-powder lacerated eyes enough to distinguish anything beyond ghostly shadows in the moonlight.

His canteen empty, he spits on his fingers, dabs at the crusted ooze, moistening, picking, prying the swollen eyelids further apart, then screws his brows into a deep frown—as if cleaning, shoving a rusted stereoscope—and in a dreamlike flash, registers bleary images of colored troops gaily hauling captured cannons, herding prisoners, realizes: *We can join the fight and take the city tonight!*

Excited exclamations, a quickening pace, clatter of bayonets against canteens, shift of cartridge boxes rippling through the ranks reflect his same excited hope.

The order to go into line of battle does not come, though.

Not then.

Not until after the might of the rebel army has time to catch up, reinforce the Johnnies that the colored troops defeated.

~~~

Their regiment, the entire Second Corps hammered in fight after fight, Thomas tramps wearily between Sarge, carrying the regimental colors, and Jake, the national, sucking his teeth against the spears of hurt blazing in his injured leg, straining not to lag behind, lose the guiding brush-brush of their shoulders against his....

~~~

Sarge's three years are up today, June 22, 1864, his duty to country and comrades done.

Unable to slip away before the regiment's ordered to tear up track from the Weldon Railroad, he feigns a severe attack of the shakes on the march, shivering to beat the band.

~~~

Alerted by Sarge's crazed twitching, Thomas turns, arms raised, to take the colors. But Sarge is shaking so hard, he near drops them, and although Thomas manages to catch hold of the flagstaff, his injured leg gives way.

As it sags, he throws his weight onto his good leg, praying: *Don't let me or the colors fall or knock anyone over.*

"REBS!" "JOHNNIES!"

At the alarm, officers' orders are bellowed, bugled, drummed; iron ramrods clink and scrape as men load and cap their pieces; a flesh-crawling yip-yip-yipping jerks Thomas's head up into blinding glare, the horror of a galloping gray tide!

Staggering like a drunk, he wrestles with jamming the butt end of the staff into the flag carrier's socket.

"Dang it to hell, keep ranks!"

Impossible when the howling stampede of gray fury is on top of them, belching deadly fire, men and horses are falling, screaming, cursing, and groaning.

Abandoning the struggle to secure the flagstaff in the carrier, Thomas slams it against his right hip for support, lopes into choking smoke, storm of buckshot and balls, clashing steel.

"Fix bayonets!"

Instantly, steel shanks of bayonets rattle on rifle barrels.

"For God's sake, come up to the front!"

Thomas, mowed down, shouts, "Save the colors," scrambles into a protective crouch over the threatened flag, whips out his jackknife to cut the remnants of silk into pieces small enough to hide against capture by the enemy.

Even as he starts slashing silk from staff, helping hands reach out from the screeching, yowling brawl. Cold steel flashes, easily shreds the worn scraps into bits and pieces that rapidly disappear.

Stuffing the final sliver deep into a pocket, he feels a stab against breastbone, shifts to get away. Instead, pointy metal rips wool, grazing skin.

With his free hand, he grabs—*a bayonet's shank? Please, God, no!*

But thick, powerfully strong fingers are wrapping around his wrist to gleeful crowing, "Looky what we got here," yanking him from his fellows, and no comrades reach out for him as they did for the colors....

HELL
July 1864 – May 1865

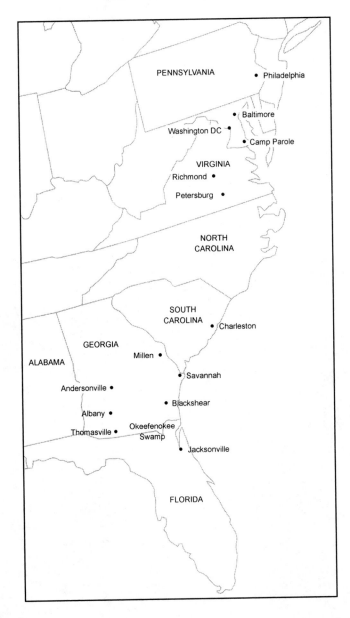

PENNSYLVANIA

• Philadelphia

• Baltimore

Washington DC •

• Camp Parole

VIRGINIA

Richmond •

Petersburg •

NORTH
CAROLINA

SOUTH
CAROLINA

• Charleston

GEORGIA

Millen •

ALABAMA

• Savannah

Andersonville •

• Blackshear

Albany •

Thomasville •

Okeefenokee
Swamp

• Jacksonville

FLORIDA

36

Stripped and bloodied, Thomas is rolled up in a tight ball of hurt against further attack from his gloating captors.

"Yi-hi, like yer tail docked?"

"Whaddya say we finish the job, he-he?"

"Yeah, geld the devil!"

No, Lord, please, no ....

~~~

Tested by the Almighty in the raucous hell of the Andersonville stockade, Matthew is stripped down to his drawers and shoes like the three cousins. His knees knocking theirs, they're hunched in their tent-fly's skimpy shade, picking lice the size of wheat kernels from their pants' seams, then cracking them dead. He's too reliant on the cousins' cunning to snap at them like he did before capture, and the boys, unchecked, buzz as irritatingly as the swarms of flies and mosquitoes they all swat. So absurd is their story of seventeen hundred Second Corps surrendering to the enemy on the Weldon Railroad, however, his disbelief slips out.

"We—Archie and me—was at the gate when three carloads of fresh fish come in," Georgi flares.

"We *saw* them," Archie confirms. "They was fought out and used up."

Rick scratches his thigh. "How yer reckon Thomas done it?"

"Thomas?" Matthew blurts in utter puzzlement. "Do what?"

"We gonna hafta say everything double?" Archie demands. "We told yer some of them fresh fish was New Yorkers what said a China-man saved their colors from capture."

"What—"

The cousins explode in derisive chortles.

"Yer don't get it!"

"Have yer seen a Chinese Yankee outside of our Thomas? No!"

"So it's gotta be him."

"Thomas got discharged for being blind," Matthew, still bewil-dered, points out.

"Dontcha remember when Lanky come back, he said Thomas wanted to get back in the fight, too?" Rick retorts. "He musta got a New York outfit to take him!"

~~~

What Matthew remembers is Lanky saying Thomas was too blind to soldier. But prisoners pouring into the stockade from the Weldon Railroad debacle affirm the captured Chinaman bears the name Thom-as Sylvanus, and the cousins want him to join their mess!

Their tent-fly, stretched over poles, barely shelters *four* from daily downpours, brutal sun, and dangerous night dews. Similarly scant is their tarpaulin ground cover without which they'd be soaked in gul-lies of wet after rain. Despite four shares in an illicit prisoner-dug well, they're always thirsty, and there's no question of drinking from the stockade's one stream: It serves as latrine for over twenty thou-sand captives; a garbage dump for the shambles of a hospital and the guards' cookhouse. Their rations are too paltry to ease the pinch and

growl of their bellies either, not even with the cousins' shrewd barter-
ing for little life-saving extras.

Appalled, Matthew croaks. "Thomas should be with his New
York comrades."

The three jump on him as one.

"Yer don't see Thomas with them now, do yer?"

"We trained together, and he woulda come back to us if he could."

"Yeah, he's one of us!"

"Family!"

~~~

Matthew mashes dead the worms crawling out of the condemned
mule meat. He doesn't care how many captives messing together call
themselves family. He can't, he *won't* use the word for the uncouth
cousins.

Admittedly, the boys have been as loyal to him as to each other.
When captured in the field, they saved his shoes as well as theirs from
barefoot Johnnies by pushing him, howling, to the ground as they dove
into steaming horse droppings, rolled in the stink, then tore the hem
off their shirts and wrapped the strips around perfectly good soles as if
they'd otherwise fall apart. They hid his penknife along with theirs inside a half-eaten loaf of moldy bread that they casually tossed between
them as they were marched from holding pen to holding pen, and they
showed him how to save his banknotes from thieving guards by fold-
ing and pressing them under the covers of his brass buttons. At his
refusal to follow their instructions for getting his ring past humiliating
body searches, they even took turns swallowing and then retrieving it.

This bounty was what the boys, once in Andersonville, used to
barter for the tent-fly, poles, tarpaulin, and shares in the well. Also,
two tin mugs, plates, and an empty coffee can for collecting and cook-

ing raw rations, a boot-top fitted with a wooden bottom for a bucket. Everything shared as in family.

There's no stopping the boys from extending this same loyalty to Thomas, and they look for him among incoming prisoners, puzzle over his prolonged absence while picking out teeth-breaking pebbles from their bean ration:

"He couldn't be imprisoned in Richmond, could he?"

"Nah, there was no room for us when we was processed there."

"Belle Isle was overcrowded, too."

"Huh, Andersonville's the biggest stockade and it's as jammed. I'll wager it got as many people as Philly."

"On account of Washington suspending prisoner exchanges because Confederates won't exchange colored soldiers for white," Matthew reminds, hoping to rouse their ire, direct it against Thomas.

"Dontcha ever listen?" Rick scolds. "We ain't talking about exchanges but Thomas."

"Yeah," Georgi says. "He gotta be coming here."

Not to us, Matthew pleads.

37

Barefoot and bareheaded, his tattered uniform hiding myriad hurts, Thomas bakes in an airless cattle car, his breathing as labored as the locomotive wheezing, rattling, thumpety-bumping over old track. Weak from countless days of gimping in hard marches without so much as a crust of bread, his only water lapped from muddy puddles after rain, he rocks dizzily, slip-slides in muck reeking of manure.

He's no longer alone or naked or an object of sport, though. Nor is he shuffling and clanking in a slave coffle as threatened. He's bobbing in an ocean of blue, and in the soft press of wool, flesh on every side, he rests at last, floating into dreams of true comrades....

~~~

Matthew's hair, turned white to its roots at Antietam, hangs to his bony shoulders in greasy snarls. His skin, scabbed from itching and clawing, has blackened under Georgia's blistering sun, soot from puny cooking fires spewing pitchy-pine smoke. Still he hasn't overcome his shock at the unearthly roar and exhalations when Andersonville's gates ground open, his terror as they slammed shut, locking him in with thousands of filthy, bearded, scraggly-haired grotesques in jumbled shanties. Indeed, many a captive has collapsed at the stockade's gates or, gaping dumbfounded, been robbed of his wits. And when the cousins, faithfully searching for Thomas among incoming prisoners,

157

return with him, Matthew can plainly see the boy shares the vacant expression of the witless.

But Chinamen are notoriously sly, and Matthew's as certain as certain can be that Thomas is neither witless nor blind but soliciting sympathy by playacting a blank-faced mute with poor sight. Sobbing in the dark of night as if in a nightmare, he makes his eyes bruised, puffy, and leaky as overripe plums, cranes his neck, swivels his head, fumbles, and trips as he did back at Harrison's Landing. He's even added a limp!

The cousins, completely taken in, fuss and cluck over the wily wretch like mother hens. When spooning for sleep, they tuck him between them, and whether off to the sinks or to collect their rations or in their shanty, one of them is at his side warning:

"Thirty feet in from the stockade wall's the deadline what nobody can see 'cause the strips of board what was the line got stolen for cooking fires."

"Poke *one* toe over the line what ain't there and the sentries posted in them boxes top of the wall will shoot to kill."

"Yankees is killing Yankees."

"Thieves is plentiful as cooties."

"Yer gotta be wary when yer walking."

"Hunch over to eat less'n yer ration be wrenched outa yer hands."

He's wrenching food out of our hands! Matthew wants to shout.

It doesn't matter that Thomas gets his own ration and, with his sly ways, has managed to insinuate himself into two white regiments. Chinese, including self-proclaimed Chinese Yankees, are colored, and since colored are blocking exchange, he's as much to blame as any colored trooper for the stockade's swollen population that's reduced rations to a cup of gritty corn meal, rice, or beans; bit of flinty cornbread; thumb-size piece of rancid bacon, rotting beef, or wormy mule meat with hair attached. As the cousins themselves put it, "Just enough to keep life in our lice and fleas."

Heaven be thanked a fellow in the Seventh Wisconsin Artillery has submitted a petition to Washington for exchange on *any* terms. Pray God, it'll be granted, and soon; meanwhile, Thomas will be recognized for the fraud he is, forced to leave this mess, and sent where he belongs—to the stockade's hundred or so colored troopers that the commandant uses for compulsory labor.

38

Sarge, captured in the Weldon Railroad shambles, wants desperately to believe the war-chin about prisoner exchanges. But three torturous months in this boiling cesspool have taught him that rumors, passed from tongue to tongue, become more exaggerated with each retelling—like the palaver about China Tom having served in a Pennsylvania outfit, the sightings of him here that evaporate like night dew.

Even so, Sarge can't resist replaying every hopeful fragment about exchange:

"Marching orders are on their way."

"The commandant is drawing up a list."

"Detachments will leave every day."

"The stockade will be empty in weeks."

Judging from the guards' threadbare uniforms, grumbles about short rations, eagerness for Yankee greenbacks and brass eagle buttons in trade, the Confederacy *has* to be buckling under the strain of feeding ever more captives. Moreover, the stockade's boiling crush of rot and disease isn't only killing skeletal captives, but scrawny guards.

So maybe the war-chin about exchange *is* accurate, and he can finally return home to his wife and son.

39

Restored to himself through the miracle of family, Thomas has understood the likelihood that his comrades, captured before him, would leave for exchange first, and he's dreaded their departure. But how could he not be glad for them!

So when the cousins dash into the shebang whooping that they're on the day's list to get out and Matthew shouts, "Hallelujah," Thomas cheers wholeheartedly.

Bidding them, "Godspeed," however, he can't stop his voice from cracking like his heart.

"Yer turn next," Georgi consoles.

"Yeah," Archie assures. "We *all* getting outa this hell."

"To give the Johnnies hell!" Rick laughs.

~~~

Thomas clings to the cousins' final buck-up as closely as he does to all they've taught him. By November, though, so many detachments have marched, hobbled, shuffled out, the stockade is eerily empty and his skin prickles in goose bumps from winter chill, mistrust of the stockade's commandant, a grizzly, pistol-wielding devil.

No prisoner-dug well can serve as a tunnel for escape. Yet weeks before exchange began, the devil stormed into the stockade alongside his hounds and their handler—the pack of them savagely snapping and snarling—to find the wells and destroy them because four captives had tunneled out.

Never mind the hounds had already hunted down the runaways, dragged them back viciously mauled to be locked in stocks where they were broiling under hot sun, their wounds crawling with flies, blood-sucking mosquitos, and maggots, their only water salty licks of sweat, night dew. As the cousins steamed at the time, "The devil ain't happy less'n he making misery."

What new misery the devil's stirring up, Thomas can't decipher. He only knows that his name has at last been called for exchange—along with every remaining captive in the stockade except the Colored Troopers the devil uses like slaves.

So until he's on the train, nay, until the train pulls out of the station, he won't believe he's on the road to freedom once more. Then, and only then, will he cheer.

~~~

To fit the stockade's remaining 841 prisoners on the train, the corporal of the guard orders one man seated on the floor with his legs drawn up, the next between the first's knees, and so firmly are they wedged that during the 200-mile journey ahead, any prisoner beyond the reach of the 2 water buckets and cracker ration placed in each boxcar will have to rely on the charity of his fellows.

Slamming the doors shut, the corporal posts two guards on top of each car to look out for—and shoot—any prisoners who, skeptical of exchange, might try to escape by throwing themselves off the train after it's underway. Finally, he gives the signal for it to pull out, and in the screeching, hissing clouds of steam, he catches a bleat of cheers, huzzahs. Most of the prisoners must still swallow the commandant's dodge that they're on their way to exchange!

You'll get your exchanges, the corporal tells them with grim satisfaction. *Yes, sirree. Not the way you were told, soldier for soldier in Savannah, but through the transformation every mortal undergoes, the way my own boy attained release from his suffering in a Yankee hell-hole. And, since death occurs on every transport, some of you will go very soon. None of you will have to wait long, though. The almanac predicts an unusually harsh winter, and the thousands of earlier transfers to Millen's stockade have already used every stick of wood and scrap of canvas available for building shelter—*

40

In the icy cold of the Millen stockade, Thomas shrinks his neck deep into his scrunched up shoulders and wraps his blanket—no, not his but the cousins' who, over his protests, insisted on swapping the best of what each was wearing for his tatters before falling into ranks to leave Andersonville:

"By tomorrow or the day after, we gonna be in Savannah."

"Exchanged and stripping off these smelly rags for burning."

"Then jumping in the Savannah River!"

"Exchange" a cruel hoax, the only jumping open to them would have been from the train between stockades. So the three are almost certainly here, near naked, shivering and shaking while he's cloaked in the blanket they bartered for when September nights turned cold. He's also wearing Archie's sleeved and buttoned jacket; Georgi's completely intact pants; Rick's left shoe, Archie's right.

Everything's become more soiled and worn in the long weeks since they were gifted. But they're still far better than anything the cousins got from him so must be returned, if at all possible before the threatened storm hits, and to this end, Thomas limps blindly around the stockade, resisting the urge to block the wind that's scalding his eyes shut, searing his nose and ears, chaffing his skin by raising the blanket from his shoulders over his head: His face must be exposed or the cousins can't see and waylay him as they did before.

On every side, there's the pitiful bawling of captives beating their fists against shanty doors, begging to be let in, anguished refusals:

"We've not an inch of room left."

"We're too many already."

Besieged by pleas to share his blanket, he apologizes:

"I can't. It's not mine to give."

"The blanket belongs to my family."

"My family needs it."

41

His blanket, clothing, and boots sodden, Thomas is soaked to the skin, chilled to the bone. Weak, too, from days of fruitless searching for family without as much as a piece of hardtack for rations. So stiff and sore after endless hours of helpless jouncing while crammed in a rocking cattle car that his legs refuse to support him. Yet his spirits soar: The hubbub of frantic citizens fleeing Savannah confirms the abrupt evacuation of the Millen stockade due to advancing Yankees!

At the prospect of rescue, his spirits stay high despite jolting to ever more remote locations in old flatcars hauled by rickety engines over rotten tracks; prisons that are merely rough ground surrounded by deep ditches too wide for even the able-bodied to jump; rations so irregular he's clawing for roots, sucking on the oozings of gum from pine. Since every difficulty he endures is another sign of the Confederacy's collapse, he considers them reason for celebration!

The Johnnies have even been sending recruiters to the prisons, overlooking the dubious fitness and loyalty of any captive willing to accept their inducements. Such desperation for soldiers surely means the war likely to end, and soon, in Union victory!

Buoyed by imminent victory, he manages to stagger through miles of pine forests and slog through waist-deep swamps. At the realization guards are ordering them onto a train for Andersonville, however, he collapses.

42

Trembling into wakefulness on a lumpy pallet, Thomas flails weakly, frantically.

Where am I?

A luminous glowing face and shimmering wash of halo and wings hover above him.

Am I dead?

Hands float down, rest feathery light on his brow, his cheek.

"Shush, there, shush. You've nothing to fear. You're in one of the hospital sheds outside the Andersonville stockade."

If I'm back in hell, this angel could be the devil!

Yet the hands are gentle in lifting his head, inserting a soft morsel between his lips.

Savoring the soothing warmth of the rapidly dissolving morsel, he recognizes bread soaked in milk, and his lips eagerly part for another....

~~~

Thomas now knows Sister John is a Daughter of Charity, the enormous white headdress of her order what he mistook for a halo and wings. To him, however, she is an angel. An angel who, given time, could restore him with her compresses for his eyes, herbal salves for his sores.

167

But since he can sop the bread in milk, eat by himself, the hospital's medical officer has ordered him back to the stockade, and his chest ridged deep as a new washboard, his belly sunk against his spine, he sinks to his knees after a few steps. Were it not for a kindly guard helping him up, gifting him with a sturdy pine branch, he'd have to crawl.

Reluctantly, he acknowledges he's as ruined for soldiering as if he were a gun thrown into a ditch of water and then stamped deep into the mud to prevent its use by the enemy.

~~~

Bitter cold, drenching rains have drummed the stockade's sand into hard clay without killing a single flea or louse, and Thomas, in hopeless attempts to stop the itching, scratches open sores scabbed over in hospital, digs more.

The cousins' blanket and shoes long gone, their jacket and pants shredded, he shakes from chill and damp even when in the shallow pit he scooped for protection. His joints ache. He's creaky as a man of ninety.

Awake and asleep, hunger gnaws like a voracious rat trapped in his belly. Yet so tender is his mouth and poorly cooked are their rations that whether he's biting down on hard grains of rice or beans floating in tepid water, his teeth wobble, the roots shoot sharp stabs of pain, and the rusty tang of blood, always present, intensifies.

A dark red throbbing behind his eyes is ever present, too, and since the lids open and shut as though scraping over broken glass, he fears what oozes out—although yellowish when smeared on his finger and viewed closely—could be blood. Bathing his eyes in water strained free of vermin and dirt through his teeth does offer momentary relief. Then every blink scrapes as excruciatingly as before.

Nothing gets rid of the troublesome grainy veil. He's been spared both the irrevocable darkness of a grave and the unrelieved blackness he suffered back in Harrison's Landing, however. And with the support of his makeshift cane, he can gimp to roll call and collect his rations in a lopsided shuffle.

For these mercies, Thomas offers daily thanks.

43

Thomas has heard war-chin about imminent exchange, rescue, and Union victory too many times to credit the renewed buzz that's been sweeping the stockade since bleak winter thawed into blustery spring.

Even when guards grind open the heavy gates and he falls into ranks to leave for prisoner exchange, memory of the devil's trickery smothers any chance of excitement.

As he thumps down his pine-branch cane and drags shakily after it, inching towards the open gates, though, hope stirs....

~~~

The matron is eager to minister to the thousand or so Yankees collapsed at the open-air feeding station for exchanged prisoners of war: In the confusion surrounding rebel surrender, the Confederacy's collapse, these poor men have been on the road to parole in Jacksonville for almost a month, tramping barefoot through forests and swamps in all sorts of weather, even circling back once to Andersonville where their journey began, and so shockingly do they resemble corpses that her handkerchief is as damp with tears as the field from April showers.

Fast as her heavy basket of sandwiches and soggy hems allow, she squelches towards the poor creatures mewling, crying for refreshment. As she nears, putrid smells assault her nostrils, grow stronger, and she has to grind her boots into the mud to keep from running. Closer, she stares in horror at the vermin crawling in and out of tangled hair, suppurating sores, rags. Instead of yanking her skirts close, however, she invokes the spirit of Jesus Christ who put forth His hand and touched a leper, then leans low and places a sandwich into the filthy claws of a creature with skin so jaundiced and eyes so swollen into slits he resembles a Chinaman....

44

After six weeks of rest and good eating in Camp Parole, Thomas's legs have strengthened so he can walk without a cane. His eyeballs have stopped screaming hurt. His eyelids' harsh grating has eased. The heavy veil screening all has thinned. Not enough, though, for him to search for comrades among the soldiers here, and none have hailed him.

Listening to excited exchanges about families, eagerly anticipated reunions, he thinks wistfully of the cousins, wonders whether, back in the embrace of their parents, brothers, sisters, they'll welcome him as they did in the stockade; whether they, too, feel strangely let down by the long awaited war's end, hard-earned Union victory.

How excited he was at his acceptance for enrollment in the Eighty-first Pennsylvania! Asked then for his day of birth, he gave July 4 to signify the freedom he'd seized in running from the Duvalls, the freedom that he believed fighting, winning the war would quickly make secure.

His first July 4 as a soldier, he lost his sight at Harrison's Landing.

By his second, he'd been Inspected, Condemned.

His third, he was in captivity.

But the next, the next he'll have mustered out, be a freedman!

Where?

Doing what?

~~~

Testing his ability to negotiate busy streets outside the camp, Thomas is abruptly halted by hands gripping both arms just below his shoulders, the sunny dazzle of grins: *The cousins?!*

"Good afternoon."

Drooping with disappointment, Thomas stares fixedly, and as the multiple images meld into one, the hands around his arms let go, the voice that greeted him booms:

"I apologize for accosting you, but I couldn't get your attention, and I trust you'll consider my reason worthy.

"You see, I've come from Connecticut to open a school for freedmen, and the room I've rented at the corner of West and Lee Streets will be ready to receive students Monday."

Fourth of July fireworks crackle inside Thomas. "Can I come to your school?"

The schoolmaster nods vigorously. "Freedmen of all ages, whether male or female, are welcome. So, please, *do* avail yourself of the opportunity, and tell your comrades and friends."

~~~

Back in camp, Thomas hurries to the surgeon for spectacles.

The surgeon, refusing the request as premature, counsels patience, "Starvation and overexposure have temporarily blinded hundreds, perhaps thousands, to varying degrees. Full restoration will take time."

"I can't wait," Thomas presses. "The school for freedmen starts Monday."

"You're a Chinaman!"

"The teacher said I'd be welcome."

"You'd take the place of a freedman?" the surgeon asks sternly.

His disapproval is clear, and Thomas, afraid the surgeon can prevent his attending the school, pours out his history—Mrs. McClintock bringing him to America for study, then falling into the hands of Dr. Mills, years of enslavement in the Duvall household, running to join the Freedom Army.

"I can't lose another chance for school, I can't."

"You won't," the surgeon assures. "But unlike most freedmen, you already have four, five years of formal education. Besides, your regiment will be mustering out in New York. I've a missionary friend in that city. He'll help you enroll in a suitable school."

TWO

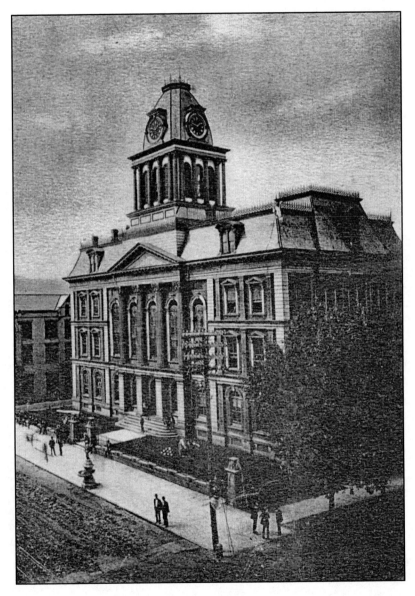

1865 - 1890

STARTING OVER
June 1865 – November 1868

45

Reverend Alexander, anxious to add luster to his small school by training a native preacher for dark China, is impatient to begin. But the Chinese Yankee, come early to Hightstown, New Jersey, for the healing properties of wholesome country food and air, is under his surgeon's orders not to attempt study before fall.

Why, Reverend Alexander can't fathom. The youth seems healthy enough, remarkably untouched by his years of soldiering.

~~~

Thomas, eager to hurry away the days until school starts, rises at cockcrow with his fellows—needy students who labor at an adjacent farm for their tuition and board. Exchanging easy banter, he pulls on trousers, shirt, and boots, joins the reverend and his wife to pray, breakfast on crisp bacon sizzling from the pan; flavorful buckwheat cakes smothered in butter and maple syrup; creamy thick milk; steaming hot coffee sweetened with honey. The myriad rich tastes dance on his tongue, and he remains at table until his belly is pleasantly full. Then, donning wide-brimmed hat, he strides across land blessedly unscarred by shells, the wheels of heavy artillery, charging soldiers.

At the peaty bogs in which cranberries are cultivated, he savors the peaceful hum of honey bees, whistles to the joyous twitter of birds as he weeds. He relishes the wonder and satisfaction of helping save plants from choking on rushes, wild grasses, allowing them to flourish.

Told cranberry plants were named for cranes, he instantly recognizes the resemblance between the birds' lengthy necks and the creeping shrubs' wiry stems. Pretending he discerns the crane's head and bill in the pink flowers, too, he delights in anticipating the moment his eyes are sufficiently restored so he really can.

~~~

In school, Thomas has to rely on general shapes to guess at words on the chalkboard. For quieting letters swimming on a page, he squeezes his eyes shut in repeated blinks, shifts the angle he's holding the book or his head, varies how closely or hard he stares. Writing, he lays his left hand flat across the paper for a line-guide. And on days there's not a whit of glare in the sunshine pouring through the windows, his teacher doesn't hurry him, or he's lucky in his guesses, his schoolwork garners praise.

Only there aren't enough such days, especially after winter storms blow in gloom too deep for gaslights to dispel, and the Reverend Alexander dismisses him for defective eyesight.

Thomas wants to plead for more time, to claim his vision is improving as promised. But the truth is that he can't see much clearer than when he left Camp Parole and spectacles don't help, rendering an education forever out of his reach.

46

Utterly dispirited, Thomas reminds himself that he made a life in Philadelphia before with neither full sight nor education, and in hopes of reclaiming it and his old comrades, he goes back.

His former landlady's welcome is so wonderfully warm it feels like a homecoming.

"I've got something for you," Mrs. McClung says, starting to ease open the hall stand's drawer, which is even more overstuffed than Thomas remembers.

Mrs. McClung seems older and frailer, too. Riffling through papers, clinking keys, her palsied fingers become entangled in long trails of string.

"Och, I know it's here," she mutters over and over.

Finally, triumphantly, she extracts an envelope, and as she hands it to him, Thomas recognizes the distinctive shapes of large lettering: *Lanky!*

His throat lumps: *This could be another invitation, "COME ROOM WITH ME."*

~~~

Margaret McClung's as effusive in her thanks to God Almighty as she was to Thomas in her welcome.

Since the factories making war goods fell silent, she's had too many empty rooms to meet her expenses. Down to a single steady lodger the week before Thomas's return, she was suffering such chill premonitions of losing her house and going begging to relatives in Pittsburgh that she shook as if palsied. Now, with income from two, she stands a fighting chance of hanging on, if only by a thread.

Her other lodger, Mr. Smith, is nearer fifty than forty; a veteran despite his age, and rightly proud of it. His tales—whether of soldiering down south or his youth in the rolling hills of Western Pennsylvania—are as colorful as the backdrops he paints for theatres. Och, the man's as gay and garrulous as young Thomas seems to have turned broody quiet!

~~~

Preparing backdrops for Smithy, Thomas covers old scenes with layers of black paint. Bits of old scenes sometimes bleed through. Similarly, deep in sleep, scenes from Lanky's letter surface.

Never of Matthew, who's alive and studying for the ministry in Philadelphia. What haunts are—

Samuel falling in the initial charge at Cold Harbor, lying trapped between the lines. Jakob recognizing his voice among the harrowing calls for help and sprinting out of the trench to retrieve him; then, knocked down by a sharpshooter, uttering three painfully strained and broken high-pitched cries: Kamarad! Stay! Trench!

Lanky bearing anguished witness as the fallen, repeatedly hit by potshots and shelling, scream and mewl and groan during the four long days and nights it took the generals to negotiate a truce for collecting the wounded and dead. His grim search for their two comrades among the exploded bodies, some still moaning; then finding them side by side, their shattered remains too decayed to separate; burying them together.

Nowhere in Lanky's letter is there an address for a response. Nor is there anything to suggest he'll write again. Yet Thomas, stepping into Mrs. McClung's hall, can never stop himself from checking the tray where she puts the day's mail, hoping against hope he'll see an envelope with his name writ large.

Out in the street, he keeps an ear cocked for a friendly halloo although he can't recall Matthew ever hailing any of them; Lanky's fled to California to start over; and the cousins, last seen leaping off a prison train in a bid for escape, failed to return to their families, so couldn't have survived. As long as he's in Philadelphia, though, Thomas knows he'll keep hoping otherwise.

47

Smithy's tales of derring-do from the war remind Thomas too much of his losses. Even Frank, his comrade from the Emergency Ninety-Day Militia, is dead, his neighbors say from the effects of Gettysburg's noxious fumes.

Smithy's comrades were his childhood friends, however, and Thomas usually manages to redirect his war stories to jolly memories of play: tossing a pigskin ball over the school house roof in games of "over-ball;" climbing wild walnut trees to shake branches free of nuts and then cracking them open with stones for the sweet meat within; setting traps of their own devising for quail and pheasants; fashioning slender rods, metal reels and hooks, casting out yards of line, whirring in perch, bass, salmon, pike.

Thomas's favorite stories are of merry making. Listening, he pictures himself joining in corn-husking jigs, winter skating parties, sleigh-rides, and frolics, wonders: *Can I?*

Certainly Smithy's vivid tales have made familiar the people of Indiana County, Pennsylvania, as well as its thickly forested hills, clear rivers, snug hollows, rich farms, and bustling townships. True, the area doesn't have any Chinese and there are very few colored—maybe a couple dozen in Indiana Borough, the county seat, none in some townships. But the entire county was strongly Union, and Smithy's been a comrade to him since the day they met.

Also, unlike Philadelphia, Western Pennsylvania isn't suffering an economic slump. In Indiana Borough, a handsome new courthouse will soon replace the old, and although the borough's unpaved streets can be so treacherous that carriage drivers risk fines for clattering along the wood sidewalks to avoid getting stuck in ruts and mud, there are taverns and inns aplenty to serve folk who stream from outlying farms and townships to its general stores, mills, harness shops, and blacksmiths as well as the quarterly court sessions.

So finding work shouldn't be hard. In fact, Smithy's oldest childhood friend, Mahan, is opening a hotel.

"Would you recommend me to Mahan for a job?"

"Consider it done!"

~~~

Once Thomas leaves, Margaret McClung will have to shut up the house that's given her a living for two decades as a widow.

Infected by his bright excitement, however, she surprises herself by saying, "Och, you're not the only one starting over. I'll be off soon to my sister-in-law's in Pittsburgh. That's just a few hours by train from Mr. Mahan's establishment in Indiana Borough. Maybe you'll visit."

185

48

Mahan's sole regret about starting over is that he didn't do it much sooner.

After rollicking years of tenting, carousing, and fierce fighting, his family farm felt like a stockade. His wife didn't like giving up her freedom in running the farm as she pleased either. As for his children: Grown into strangers while he was gone, they didn't warm to him any more than he to them. Still he tried to stick it out. But this spring, his sap rose strong as in the big sugar maples and he busted out for frolics with tavern maids, inn-keeping in Indiana Borough.

To attract old soldiers to his hotel, he's called it the Union and offers the best liquor, eating, and stabling in the borough. What really puts his Union Hotel at the top of the heap, however, is his Chinese general utility man.

Mahan pours himself a congratulatory drink of rum. It's no secret he's not partial to foreigners any more than the rest of the county, which is mostly Scotch-Irish like him. But Thomas isn't one of those filthy, pigtailed rat-eaters driving honest, hardworking white men out of jobs in California; he's a veteran. The only Chinese in the Union Army! As much of a curiosity as Barnum's midget: General Tom Thumb.

Why, folks from all over the county come to gawp at the Union Hotel's Chinese Yankee. And, of course, many a man then drifts into the taproom to quench his thirst and return to the boisterous camaraderie of the war, the chance to flirt with pretty barmaids. Understandably reluctant to go back to their dull lives, they then decide to stay overnight, sometimes—if they get lucky as he has—with a chambermaid.

~~~

His mistake, Thomas realizes, was assuming that since Smithy and Mahan were childhood friends as well as comrades, they'd share similar natures. His employer is, in fact, a swaggering, hard drinking, womanizing braggart who makes him feel as much a jape as if he were a costumed celestial doorman.

Not surprisingly, Mahan's fellow drunks and womanizers follow his lead for the sake of free drinks and liberties with the serving maids in the taproom, bed chambers. Thomas nonetheless doesn't regret coming.

In the six months since his arrival, the calls of "Look, the Chinaman," demands to "Talk Chinese!" and relentless quizzing that used to plague him while stabling horses, lugging coal from the cellar, serving in the taproom, and cleaning tobacco quid from its floor have steadily faded, almost gone. In their place, he enjoys camaraderie from most in the taproom; greetings on the street; even, occasionally and flickeringly, the sensation of victory that was missing directly after the war ended.

To his surprise, despite Indiana County's strong support for the Union during the war, not everyone here backs General Grant for president in the November elections. Fast as the Republican committee whips out flags, banners, and portraits of Grant, the Democrats send up larger flags, post unflattering caricatures.

In the Union's smoky taproom, liquored voices warn:

"Republicans will give Negroes the vote."

"Protect the rights of white men by sticking to the Democratic ticket!"

Thomas, determined to vote for the general who helped secure his freedom, decides to go to the Federal Courthouse in Pittsburgh and file his papers for citizenship.

~~~

October 29, 1868 is a date Will shan't forget. A clerk in Pittsburgh's Federal Courthouse for almost a decade, he assists aliens petitioning for naturalized citizenship, and contrary to the usual parade of German and Irish, sprinkling of French or English, he's got a petitioner rare as a meteorite, a veritable celestial phenomenon that's set his head jangling over conflicting laws.

The Act of July 17, 1862 promises naturalization to any honorably discharged foreign veteran upon his petition; but the 1790 Federal Statute specifically restricts the right to "any alien, being a free white person;" and neither the 1866 Civil Rights Act, which accords long overdue citizenship to Negroes, nor the Fourteenth Amendment, finally ratified this July, includes Celestials.

Yet there's nothing offensive about the one here. A neatly groomed youth, he's responded to every question with native-born fluency and utmost courtesy, produced proof of honorable discharge, and is accompanied by his former landlady, a respectable elderly woman in rusty black who has volubly testified to his good moral character while showing off a carte de visite of him in uniform holding battle-proud national colors.

Breaking into an icy sweat, Will grips his pen as fiercely as a sword, presses his arms flat against the desktop to prevent their shaking, and begins filling out a petition, his usually perfect lettering helter-skelter, his mind leaping ahead of his galloping heart to what comes next—a District Court judge ceremonially swearing in the Petitioner, presenting him with a Certificate of Naturalization.

Will a judge swear in this Celestial?

Not in this courthouse.

But I'm the one who makes out Certificates of Naturalization, so I could complete one and give it to him, then record the citizenship granted in the Court Register.

Dare I?

Say I do and someone notices "Hong Kong, China" in the space for "nativity," I'd be embroiled in an investigation that can only end badly for the Petitioner and me both.

Thomas Sylvanus is a good Irish name, though.

I can write, "Ireland"....

49

Thomas thrills at the papers in his pocket testifying he's a true blue Chinese Yankee. But he knows citizenship doesn't guarantee a man the vote or he and his comrades couldn't have helped keep Maryland in the Union by forcing voters to walk an armed gauntlet to the polls, frightening away citizens clutching secession ballots. To better the odds for casting *his* ballot, he carefully tucks it out of sight.

The fight for Negro franchise yet raging, he could still be stopped from voting for being colored. Fortunately, the November day is glaringly bright, cold, and windy, allowing him to pull his cap low on his brow, wrap his muffler up half his face, as any sensible man would, before setting off.

Plunging into the dauntingly noisy, boisterous crowd around the polling place on the corner of Clymer and Water streets, he's thankful for his precautions. Even through his muffler, he can smell the liquored breath of Republicans and Democrats shouting slogans, roughnecks yelling threats, and to make any headway towards the voting window, he's got to push, shove, elbow, and stomp hard as those ahead of him.

No, harder.

As he vies for supremacy over those cutting into the raucous mess, fisticuffs break out between hoodlums, and he has to dodge and duck repeatedly to avoid inadvertent blows. Leastways, the troublemakers are too preoccupied with each other to single him out!

From the Maryland election, he's anticipated three Election Judges seated behind a voting window, under which will be a platform about a yard wide and a foot high that voters must mount to present their papers for approval to cast their ballots. No sooner does he tilt his head back so as not to trip while climbing onto the platform, however, a pair of Volunteer Challengers flanking the window blindside him, booming:

"It's the Chinaman!"

"Colored!"

"Foreigner!"

"Not twenty-one!"

"Not qualified to vote!"

Lickety-split so many take up the Challengers' condemnations, the Election Judge's, "Name?" is all but drowned. Beneath his feet, the platform is tipping alarmingly from rough jostling. Fingers brush his legs and arms, tug at the ends of his muffler.

Prancing, leaping, twirling to elude their grasp, he pulls out his discharge and naturalization papers, thrusts them through the window to the Election Judges while hollering above the racket, "Thomas Sylvanus, citizen, born in China July 4, 1845!"

Some close enough to hear burst into laughter.

"Our nation's birthday!"

"The Chinaman really is a Yankee!"

"A dancing Yankee!"

"Look at that fancy footwork!"

The two Volunteer Challengers—bobbing up and down alongside him as he kicks and jumps on the jouncing platform—careen so near that their fiery breath itches and burns his ears:

"Slanty-eyed!"

"Chink-Nigger!"

"No beard!"

"Not a whisker!"

"Underage!"

From behind the window, the three Election Judges belt their decision as one: "Citizen! Over twenty-one! Qualified to vote!"

Jubilantly, Thomas whips out his ticket for President and Vice-President, hands it in for himself, his dead comrades.

Then, taking back his documents, he determinedly pockets his past together with his papers and, tipping his cap at the Judges within, the Challengers on either side, moves on....

MOVING ON
1869

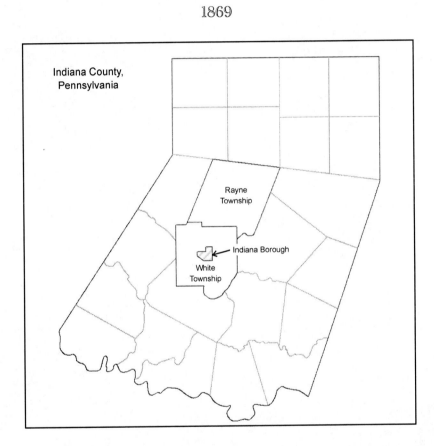

Indiana County,
Pennsylvania

Rayne
Township

Indiana Borough

White
Township

50

The Earhart hotel where Thomas is working as hostler enjoys a reputation as a family establishment. To his pleasure, its proprietors treat those who work for them as family, too, and he's reluctant to recommend Margaret Brocken, a boisterous chambermaid from the Union Hotel.

Away from Mahan and his fellow womanizing drunks, though, Margaret might well be quieter, and with the Union padlocked by debtors, she needs a job. So Thomas puts in a good word for her.

~~~

Margaret's corseted tight as is possible and still breathe. But there's no hiding either her swelling belly or her lack of a character reference, and the self-righteous prig Earhart is glowering down his nose at her like she's a speck of dirt, sniffing, "Ours is a reputable establishment. We have nothing here for the likes of you."

Then the High Constable—doubtless spurred by Mr. Self-Righteous Prig—is hauling her over the coals for loose morals, demanding, "Who's the father?"

As if either of them cares except to shame her and get the county off the hook for her support and the babe's!

But support—whether from the county or her babe's married father—isn't enough.

No.

What she wants is legitimacy for her unborn child and respectability for herself, which means she's going to get someone, not just anyone neither, but a responsible, good-hearted fellow, to marry her.

~~~

Joseph Thompson's clients in fornication and bastardy cases have included friends who are church members, leaders in the community, but regardless of personal connection or social standing, whether the distraught individual is the woman left in the lurch, the accused, or the father whose daughter or son is in trouble, his counsel has never varied. And when mild-mannered Thomas blunders in with hair wild, nostrils flared, face scarlet as the maples outside the office window, spluttering about a chambermaid from the bankrupt Union Hotel threatening to swear a false oath on him, Joseph calmly follows his usual course: He shepherds Thomas into one of the wing-back chairs for clients, then returns to his own behind his desk and, once seated, advises, "Settle quietly."

"Settling would confirm guilt!" Thomas blazes.

"No," Joseph corrects firmly. He raises both hands as a signal against further interruption. "As a relative newcomer, you probably don't realize a man is helpless against a woman's oath. A mere accusation is sufficient to condemn him."

He brings his fingertips together like the steeple of the First Presbyterian Church where they both attend services. "Our Heavenly Father knows the truth about you and the necessity for pragmatism in such cases. In yours, I suggest offering to cover the expenses for this chambermaid's lying-in—plus a little extra, if you have it—contingent on her swearing to complete silence."

"But Margaret Brocken's a bold-faced liar!"

"Neverthe—"

"What's to stop her from breaking any promise she makes?"

"Nothing," Joseph concedes. "Should she carry out her threat and swear under oath she's pregnant with your child, though, a same-day warrant will be issued for your arrest."

Thomas shoots to his feet. "I won't be blackmailed for a wrong I didn't commit. I'll go to jail first."

~~~

Recalling his client's honest indignation, Joseph sighs. Jail's where Thomas's indignation landed him and where he'd still be but for his release on bond until the December Court Sessions.

Joseph heaves another, deeper sigh. By then the child will be born, and while its racial characteristics can prove Thomas innocent of bastardy, they can't clear him of the fornication charge.

~~~

Thomas refuses to buckle under the shame of arrest, public disgrace. But he reluctantly acknowledges that until he's cleared of wrongdoing, his presence on staff would ruin the reputation of any decent establishment. So he makes no attempt to return to his position as hostler at the Earharts or seek another job in town.

Yet work he must. His case won't come to trial for seven long weeks!

Is there any place in the county beyond the reach of gossips' tongues?

A distant farm, perhaps?

197

The memory of working on the New Jersey cranberry farm wash-es over him like a balm, and with no other road open, he sets out in hope of joining the ranks of roving day laborers.

At the fields of ripe corn on every side, his heart lifts.

Surely farmers with crops ready for harvest can't afford to be any more particular about the men they take on than army recruiters....

51

Harvest time brings needed work, Henrietta grants. But she's pushing fifty, toiling under eagle-eyed, sharp-tongued farmers' wives, and every day is an eternity of sweltering over steaming kettles, stirring and bottling bounty from kitchen gardens, cooking for gangs of laborers.

She wants better for her sweet-sixteen Mattie. So, yes, there's no question Chinese Tom, a new face amidst this season's corn pickers, is entertaining, never too parched or worn to liven evenings with rollicking songs and yarns. But there are farmers' sons as charming—and far better looking, their eyes honestly round instead of crooked slits; noses shapely, not flat; skin fair, not dark.

Mattie, with her golden curls, eyes blue as a summer sky, complexion carefully kept creamy white by working indoors, hands not yet roughened but soft as a lady's, could easily snag a first-born son that'll inherit. Then she'd be giving orders to hired girls instead of taking them, and Henrietta scolds, "You should be making sheep's-eyes at the farmers' sons, not a wolf awaiting trial!"

"Margaret Brocken's a slut!"

"Watch yourself or folks will be saying that about you," Henrietta warns.

~~~

To Mattie, the fires of hell can't be more punishing than those in a kitchen, and she wants no part of housewifery as hired girl *or* wife.

No part of country living either.

What sets her blood tingling is cities.

Pittsburgh, Philadelphia, Washington....

The very names excite, and listening to Tom's tales, Mattie's heart races, floods with desire. Her feet itch.

Hook him, and city life will be hers.

~~~

For Thomas, the past weeks have been as unexpectedly refreshing as the dippers of vinegar sling—spring water mixed with vinegar and sugar—that pickers drink in the field to dispel the relentless heat, choking dust. The jovial evenings of storytelling and song, kind attentions of Mattie are so like what he dreamed for himself while listening to Smithy's tales of Indiana that, for an hour, two, three, he escapes the full weight of shameful accusation, looming public trial, possible imprisonment....

~~~

The table groans under the weight of heaped platters that Henrietta's setting out for supper at tonight's corn-husking bee. Fearful her girl is being gulled into ruination, Henrietta all but groans herself.

Warily she watches Chinese Tom seize an ear with one dusky hand, grasp multiple husks, strands of pale silk in his other. As he tears back, peeling away layer after layer, exposing juicy kernels, his slit eyes glow, stripping her poor Mattie, who's ladling out sweet lemonade.

Laughing like the very devil, Chinese Tom casts the bared cob aside. His fingers flying, he begins on the next. Henrietta, glimpsing blood-red, claps a hand over her lips to keep from crying out loud.

~~~

The rarity of a red ear of corn entitles the husker to kiss a girl of his choice, and Thomas stares disbelievingly at the rows upon rows of dark red kernels on the one he's shucking: What he's seeing must be from wishing or because his eyes hurt from grit and dust.

His heart thumping loud and fast as the cobs landing in bushel baskets from the huskers around him, he shuts his eyes, opens them: Red.

His fingers, clutching husks and silk, splay open, and in the sudden quiet, his left hand, clenching the cob, burns as if he were holding a hot poker. He almost drops it—*should* drop it: Any girl he kisses will be irrevocably stained.

Yet longing for the shimmering golden-haired Mattie tightens his grip—even in the absence of the good natured flirting, teasing, chaffing that has previously been showered on men lucky enough to be husking a red ear, even as the strange quiet turns stony....

52

Mattie wastes no time wheedling Tom into marrying her, even convincing him to take her to a justice of peace in the borough so she can show him off to relatives and friends in town.

What fun she'll have parading through the streets in new dresses, winning the admiration of dandies!

~~~

When posting bond for Thomas a month ago, Joseph Thompson never imagined his guileless client would fall prey to a second female schemer, adding to the challenge of saving him from the first.

Frustrated in the extreme, Joseph slams the marriage announcement he drafted onto his desk, commands Thomas, seated across from him, to hold his tongue and listen.

At his hurt expression, Joseph softens, but maintains a stern demeanor, tone for Thomas's own good. "Your trial next month will be as serious for you personally as any battle you fought in the war, the outcome as uncertain. Strategy is critical, which is why I wrote 'Chinese Tom' in your marriage announcement."

Sensing Thomas bristle, stiffen his neck, Joseph impales him in a steely glare. "Thomas Sylvanus is the name on your legal documents. But for people to connect 'Thomas Sylvanus' in the marriage announcement with you, people must have beside it what you're generally known by in the county—the Chinaman or Tom Chinaman or China Tom or Chinese Tom. The whole point of announcing your marriage in the newspaper is to inform the general public, particularly potential jurors at your trial, that the girl they see on your arm isn't another pert young hussy you've taken up with willy-nilly—"

"She—" Thomas, his face purpling with rage, explodes.

Joseph, raising his voice, overrides him. "She's your wife. Make that clear to people for *her* sake if not your own."

"Alright. For Mattie."

~~~

Indiana Weekly Messenger
November 24, 1869
Married
Nov. 11, by Esquire Thos. McClar-
ren, Mr. Thomas Sylvanus (Chinese
Tom) late of Philadelphia, to Miss
Mattie Woolweaver, of White town-
ship.

~~~

Mattie, crowing delightedly, cuts the announcement from the paper, turns the clipping over, brushes on paste, and positions it on the cover of the scrap book she's bought for souvenirs of their travels: *Now that Tom and I are married, Margaret Brocken can't have him even if she does win in court. So she and her baby would be better off if she goes some place where she's not known as a slut and can pass as a widow. Then Tom will be off the hook for support and we can quit the county, too!*

53

Thomas all but bursts with love for Mattie, her sweet trust in his innocence. Even now, months after sheriffs have scoured the county and failed to find Margaret Brocken, his Mattie loyally insists that his win by default is the same as if a jury, having had the chance to hear his accuser examined and see the baby, pronounced him not guilty.

But it isn't, or there wouldn't be a gossipy buzz on the streets, in shops, at church, wherever he and Mattie walk arm-in-arm. Nor would he still be relegated to farm labor, his eyes subjected to stinging grit and dirt, a return of infections both painful and blinding.

"Let's go away," Mattie urges.

"Only cowards skedaddle," he tells her.

"You're no coward," she comes back stoutly, throwing her arms around him and nuzzling his neck. "You're my Chinese Yankee."

~~~

Since six months of wheedling hasn't got Tom close to the train station, Mattie realizes she has to change tactics.

But when she runs home to family, she has to endure her mother's, "You should have listened to me, too late to come crying now." Tom's, "Of course you miss your family," is even harder to stomach.

His wanting to start a family together is worse!

Maybe jealousy will do the trick....

~~~

Sick with jealousy at Mattie going buggy riding with other men, Thomas tries the kindly sailor's trick for seasickness, "Keep your eyes on the horizon."

Mattie birthing a baby, our baby, the three of us family....

He shows her the happiness that could be theirs by moving them to Rayne Township, renting a room in the same house as the most loving of families: Martha and David Crookshank and their three lively boys.

~~~

Martha Crookshank wishes her husband, a few years shy of fifty, could hide his failing sight from employers the way Tom does: Where milky cataracts cloud David's eyes, however, Tom's eyes are bright as shiny black buttons. Except when inflamed—then they swell red, turn weepy, even ooze puss. He manages to get about alright anyway, mind, *and* to put in a full day's labor.

Unlike his wife, whose only labor is preening, swishing and flouncing her skirts, stitching a ribbon or bit of lace on a bonnet, completely ignoring her husband's clothes in need of patching and washing. She won't even rise from bed at cockcrow to start a fire so he can wake to the smell of brewing coffee, set off for the fields strengthened by several strong cups, a heaping bowl of hot mush in his belly.

That Mattie was flighty as a girl, and she's flighty now, running off to play with men in the hills all day, leaving no dinner for Tom, no water for a quick, cooling wash when he and David drag in hot and sweaty at noon. Wasn't for David inviting him to sit down at table with their family, Tom would return to the fields hungry.

205

Clanking a pail to fetch milk in the evening, Mattie's gone for hours on shameful trysts, and Tom, limping from exhaustion, can't chase after her. Wasn't for David sending their oldest boy to fetch her, the wanton would stay out the whole night.

Betimes she does anyway—for days, weeks, even months.

TESTIMONY
1874 - 1877

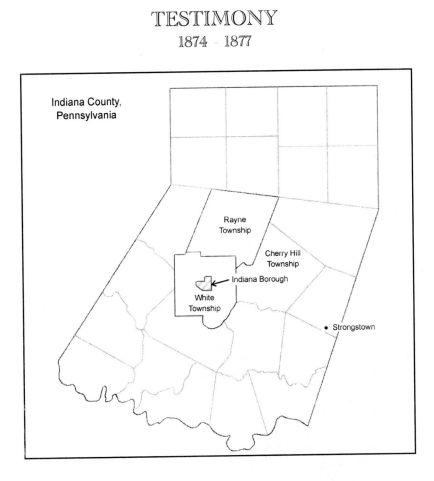

Indiana County,
Pennsylvania

Rayne
Township

Cherry Hill
Township

Indiana Borough

White
Township

• Strongstown

54

The judge would defend to his death the principle of innocent until proven guilty and that applies to judgments in petitions for divorce on the grounds of desertion.

Certainly the petitioner, Thomas Sylvanus, is the very picture of dejection: wan, shoulders hunched as though he were closer to fifty than thirty. But he's doubtless been coached by his lawyer, and the judge intends to scrutinize the testimony submitted.

There are, he sees, two witnesses: Mary Carter, a middle-aged chambermaid; and Martha Crookshank, whose family shared a house with the couple.

Both women enjoy unimpeachable reputations in the county, and they've known the wife since she was a girl, the husband since his arrival in the borough, so their testimony should be fair.

Fair but shocking: Interviewed separately by a court-appointed commissioner, each witness claims that in almost five years of marriage, husband and wife have cohabited less than one!

Furthermore, both witnesses blame the wife who, during her rare times home, didn't lift a finger to light a fire or cook a meal, not even when her husband fell ill. Instead, she passed her days in the woods "swinging on grape vines," going on buggy rides, and "wrestling" with strange men, often staying out until ten, eleven o'clock at night.

The first time this pepper-pot slipped her traces, she emptied their dwelling of its simple furnishings, pots and kettles, utensils—everything except the husband's clothes. Yet the husband, a Union veteran and model of sobriety and industry, remained loyal to her, not only then, but since, giving her money from his meager earnings as a farm laborer to "dress pretty," coaxing her to come back a day, a week, a month before she'd again run away!

~~~

Thomas is counting on his petition for divorce, which includes a subpoena for Mattie to appear in court, to return her to him, and he strains to catch the click of her heels, her scent as she hurries into court, lilting in breathless little pants, "Tommy Tom-Tom! I'm back! I've come back for good!"

~~~

The judge can't recall ever reaching a decision on a divorce petition so quickly. He only regrets that in granting the petition, he can't make an exception to the law, and he instructs Thomas Sylvanus that five years will have to pass before the divorce decree is final.

~~~

To bear the unbearable, Thomas pushes himself to the limits of his strength, then pushes some more, clearing land of roots and stumps for new fields; planting, picking, and husking corn; thrashing harvested wheat stalks with a flail, pitching off the straw, shoveling the grain into bags.

Alone on his straw tick at night, sleep still doesn't come easily. His heart beating a melancholy taps, he courts its solace, the possibility of his golden Mattie flying to his side as she did that magical evening of the red corn when she blessed him with her public declaration of love in a tender kiss.

Just the memory raises his spirits. His blood thrums. And, oh, the nights her fragrance heralds her arrival. Once again, then, he tastes her sweetness, feels the silky softness of her hair, petal-smooth skin. His heart takes wing, soars—

55

In the doctor's view, medicine alone is inadequate for veterans like Thomas Sylvanus.

His constitution irreparably weakened by hard soldiering, he's barely thirty yet has twice been bedridden for months—congestion of the lungs in '73, an apoplectic attack in '75—and what saved him on both occasions wasn't doctoring so much as wholesome food and careful nursing from the worthy Martha Crookshank. Now, exhaustion has choked the veteran into gasping uselessness.

"Your body can't tolerate the punishment of daily labor," the doctor warns Thomas gravely, "and as a disabled veteran, you're entitled to an invalid pension, which would give you relief."

~~~

Thomas hacks hoarse acknowledgement. But neither his bad chest nor his apoplexy qualify as war disabilities, and he's already been denied an invalid pension for his cataracts.

There *is* his leg injury from his fall in Cold Harbor. For years, he only limped when he got really tired. Then, while suffering congestion of the lungs in '73, the old sore ulcerated. Ever since, each time his chest congests, the sore breaks open and throbs hotly, making him limp severely. But this disability would have to be claimed through his service as a substitute, and in exposing he lied under oath to the Board of Enrollment in New York, he'd throw into doubt his *every* statement.

His eye injury, on the other hand, is the indisputable reason for his discharge from the Eighty-first Pennsylvania back in '62, and with each passing year, he's endured more infections, so even on his best days, now, he's squinting and staring harder, more reliant on cues from smell, touch, sounds....

～～～

From experience, Thomas knows there's no guarantee of success in having an agency willing to submit a claim on his behalf in the expectation a pension will be granted, fees deducted from the first payment. And the Bureau of Pensions apparently now requires so many notarized affidavits that just getting them can take months. There are also thousands of claimants, and so overwhelmed are the Bureau's clerks, they sometimes fail to respond in less than a year. Even then, the reply is often a request for more affidavits or notification the claim will have to be investigated.

Compared to what the Agency must accomplish, his own search for work pales. Still it's a challenge. Hard physical labor is out of the question. Something like the light cleaning that Jackson, a disabled colored trooper, does for a sympathetic lawyer would be ideal. But Jackson got that job soon after the war when patriotism still ran high and times were good. Neither is true anymore.

56

The clerk at the Bureau of Pensions, a government girl hired when the war created a shortage of men, counts herself lucky that she wasn't among the many forced to surrender their positions to returning veterans. She finds clerical duties tedious nonetheless, and she eases her boredom by plundering the claims that cross her desk for characters and incidents she can use in the blood and thunder thrillers she scribbles late into the night.

Today's pickings have been uninspiring. So although quitting time is minutes away, she opens a new claim, turns to the Examining Surgeon's Certificate for Applicant no. 13,653.

"Thomas Sylvanus (Chinese)." *A Chinese Yankee?*

Eagerly she scans his description: "height, 5 ft 4½ in.; weight, 130 lbs.; complexion, yellow."

Her fingers flying at the prospect of a real-life sensation tale, she flips to the Adjutant General's report, dated March 7, 1877, for the Chinese Yankee's service and disability in the Eighty-first Pennsylvania Voluntary Infantry, Company D.

The sketch is disappointingly brief and dull: only sixteen months of service from enrollment to disability discharge; the action in the Peninsular Campaign a mere list of battles.

Nor do any of the thirteen testimonies distinguish the soldier as Chinese. In fact, the sole mention is in the Examining Surgeon's Certificate. And, more critically for the claimant, the testimonies don't

214

appear to support his claim for a "disability resulting from disease of eyes."

Have I missed something?

In the escalating buzz of talk, clatter and bang of drawers, chairs, and doors, she can hardly think. Or maybe it's her impatience to go home and start scribbling a tale of lurid intrigue and blood-curdling deviltry that is making focus such a challenge.

Quickly she shuffles through the sheaf of testimonies again in search of exotic details for the sensation story humming in her head, support for the Chinese Yankee's claim.

That he suffers from a disease of the eyes is incontestable. Records from the War Office include treatment for conjunctivitis. There's also a veteran who swears he witnessed the claimant's near blindness while the fellow was awaiting a disability discharge and his vision hasn't improved since. The Examining Surgeon testifies to the claimant's "constant pain" and inability to see distinctly on account of eyes that are "much inflamed." The family doctor's diagnosis is "cataract to such an extent that he cannot perform manual labor." Affidavits from some acquaintances attest to "very bad eyesight," "betimes almost blind," too. But others swear his squinting is due to his being Chinese, nothing more.

Nowhere can she find a single exoticism to color scribbling!

Nor does any of the testimony prove the claimant's disease of the eyes is a war disability rather than an affliction from which he suffered before enrollment.

57

To be alive is to be afflicted by troubles, Martha reckons, and she punches the raised dough, releasing her pent-up fury at the smooth-talking rake that got her nineteen-year-old Cousin Tillie in the family way by promising marriage, then refused to honor his pledge, slandering, "There's no proof the baby is mine. So many men might have been responsible."

Working the edges of the flattened dough to the center, Martha prays she won't regret trading on her own spotless reputation to get Cousin Tillie a position in Indiana. Quick, neat-handed, and diligent, the lass will doubtless perform her duties faultlessly, and maids in respectable households aren't permitted followers. But there's never any guarantee of safety from masters, and a raven-haired, rosy-cheeked Irish beauty is as bound to attract rakes here as in Cherry Hill.

Martha reaches into the flour bin, lightly dusts her hands for a second kneading. Having witnessed Thomas's misery over Mattie's shenanigans—

Thomas! He's back as porter at the Earhart Hotel, so will be directly across the road from Cousin Tillie.

Would a word in his ear help prevent further trouble?

Certainly he's trustworthy, and although he failed to keep Mattie from going astray, Cousin Tillie is neither deliberately wicked nor flighty like that hussy, just regrettably innocent.

~~~

From the moment Ma yelled at her for getting knocked up, Tillie prayed night and day for the blessing of the Holy Mother who got Joseph to marry her and raise Baby Jesus. But the father of her darling skulked away and Pa shouted he wasn't supporting a bastard.

Then no family in Cherry Hill would hire a disgraced girl, forcing her to take a job where no one knows about her mistake, and Indiana Borough is *miles* and *miles* and *miles* away, too far for her to go back home to suckle Baby Sadie.

Her painful, milk-swollen breasts leak, soaking rags instead of feeding her darling, and drowning in milk and longing and worry, Tillie can't make beds, wield dust cloth or sweeper without stopping to muffle sobs in soft feather ticks and pillows, thick folds of velvet curtain.

Polishing brass, she rubs like the dickens for a genie to appear.

~~~

Asked by Martha to check on Tillie, Thomas doesn't hesitate. The Crookshanks have been his truest friends. Soon, though, he's calling on Tillie for her own goodhearted self.

He marvels at how her every thought is for her baby, her fatherless baby that she welcomed and loves, never mind how people look down on her and her baby, call them ugly names.

Was I my mother's darling? Was I torn from her like Baby Sadie from Tillie?

Certainly Baby Sadie is as much of an orphan as he was.

Unless—

Can I be Baby Sadie's father?

Can Baby Sadie, Tillie, and I be family?

217

At the very possibility, Thomas's heart quickens. All he remembers of his childhood is his ache for family, a mother as fiercely loving as Tillie, a father like the kindly sailor.

But whether he's looking at Tillie through a haze thick or thin, he sees she's as beautiful as everyone says. Moreover, where she's not yet twenty, healthy and strong, he's past thirty and broken.

Would she accept me?

~~~

Tillie's heart opens to the kindly genie that has offered to restore her darling Sadie to her, give them a home.

What Tillie can't grasp is why he wants to wait.

"Baby Sadie is crying for me now," she sobs, "and my milk is drying up."

~~~

Thomas doesn't want to hold back from making a family, a home any more than Tillie. But there's been nary a word from the Bureau of Pensions about his invalid petition.

True, his duties as a porter at the Earhart Hotel are manageable when he's well, and Mr. and Mrs. Earhart accept his lapses on those occasions his eyes are infected. They'll still have to let him go, though, if his chest congests and the sore on his leg ulcerates, driving him to bed: They have a business to run.

As it is, their hotel is threatened by the ever diminishing number of travelers as bad times deepen into what some say is the worst depression the country has ever experienced. So if he loses his position at the Earharts, he'll be unlikely to find *any* work.

Moreover, his divorce won't be final until June 17, 1878.

"We can't legally marry for another eight months."

"I don't care," Tillie declares, as she has to his every concern.

How brave she is! As brave as the comrades in Andersonville who had next to nothing, yet made families together. The cousins, in stretching their little to include him, hadn't held back. Even Matthew didn't.

"Maybe I can hire a wagon so we can go to Strongstown, where neither of us is known, and find a justice of peace to marry us."

~~~

Bouncing in the rackety hired wagon, Tillie's heart dances to the merry clip-clop of the horses' hooves; Thomas, seated beside her, whistles to their beat.

The rising sun, casting a warm glow, has burned off the ashy mist, revealing dense woods dappled in golds, oranges, and reds dazzling as the pretty dress Thomas gave her, saying, "A new dress for our new life."

Unable to contain her giddy swirls of happiness, Tillie leans against Thomas, rests her head on his shoulder, starts humming the tune for the *Rock-a-bye* lullaby.

His fingers lace hers, squeeze understanding, and he sings:

"Sadie is drowsing

Cozy and fair

Mother sits near

In her rocking chair

Forward and back

The cradle she swings

And though Sadie sleeps

She hears her Pa sing."

HOME
1877 - 1883

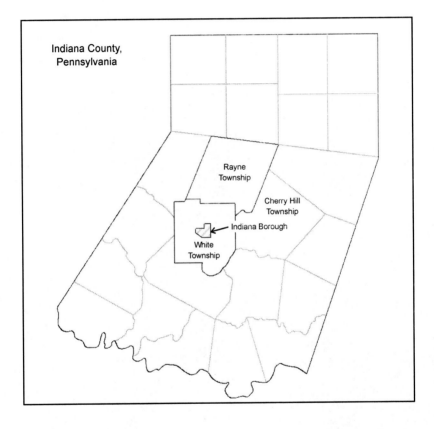

Indiana County,
Pennsylvania

Rayne
Township

Cherry Hill
Township

Indiana Borough

White
Township

58

Whether cradling a joyfully babbling Sadie in his arms, dandling her on his knees, teaching her to say, "Mama," and "Papa," or breathing in her milky fragrance while nuzzling her silky hair, Thomas is suffused with the deep contentment he's yearned for since childhood.

Tillie, freed from working outside their home, hums all the while she's mothering their daughter, cooking, doing housework. Never idle for a moment, she turns over his worn collars and cuffs; knits him mufflers, socks, gloves. And as one year unfurls into another and another, she stitches bigger dresses, smocks for their growing girl—then a receiving blanket for the new baby growing under her heart.

~~~

Thomas surprises Little Sadie with big wood alphabet blocks he's made nights while she slept.

"Mine?" she gasps in delight.

"Yours," he assures, spreading them out on the rag rug Tillie finished the morning of Baby Ellen's birth.

Reveling in her pleasure, he shows Little Sadie the black letters he's painted on each side, how each makes a different sound.

She's as attentive as if he were demonstrating magic.

Thomas marvels at how easily and enthusiastically Little Sadie learns. In a matter of months, she's memorized the entire alphabet, and when he starts grouping blocks together, she claps, crowing, "A new game!"

Today, he assembles BAA, reminds, "Baa like a sheep."

Instead of parroting him as before, Little Sadie snatches the "B." She replaces it with "W."

"WAA like Baby Ellen," she giggles.

Laughing, he turns the "W" around to make "M" and then removes one "A."

"MA," she calls out gleefully.

Her hand darts, lands on a block that she grabs too fast for him to register the letter. She places it beside the "A" he discarded and, hurling herself into his arms, exults, "PA!"

Hugging her, savoring her warm affection, absolute trust, he gazes over at the shimmering glow of Tillie and Baby Ellen, nursing in noisy bliss, prays he won't ever fail his family.

59

Laid off from the hotel, Thomas chops firewood, lugs bricks and mortar up ladders, digs cellars, hauls loads of dirt.

His eyes inflame from the dust and grit. His chest congests from exertion, harsh weather, laming his leg. Too often, he's pinned to bed. Or, no matter how many doors he raps, he can't find work, and although Baby Ellen's still nursing, Tillie takes in washing.

Helping Tillie, he falls back into the skills that the washerwomen at Newark's General Hospital patiently taught him by placing their hands over his: operating a wringer for sheets, towels; distinguishing the weight of irons by heft, their heat by the volume of sizzle from sprinkles of water; applying the perfect amount of starch on shirt fronts, collars and cuffs by touch. And when he stirs the wash in cauldrons of boiling water, the steamy warmth eases the almost constant throbbing of his eyes and head.

He used to feel the same relief in the lovely moist dimness of the hospital laundry. What bliss if he could find such employment!

Any steady work would be wonderful.

So would finally getting the four dollars a month half-pension that the Examining Surgeon recommended over a year ago: Then he and Tillie could buy a small flock of laying hens and sell the eggs; maybe even hold back some eggs for hatching, raising chickens for sale as well.

At least the Bureau of Pensions has finally notified the agency handling his case that it's sending an investigator to interview his sworn witnesses....

~~~

The chief of the Investigation Division fully recognizes the impact that decisions on pension claims have on invalid soldiers. Indeed, the burden of responsibility has stooped his shoulders, hollowed his cheeks, chest. Yet instead of resigning, as his wife pleads, the chief adds reviewing the most problematic claims to his duties.

This morning, he's been studying the file of Thomas Sylvanus, starting with the instruction given the investigator: "Gather evidence regarding claim disease of eye from war."

Remarkably, having plowed through every affidavit from the four days that the investigator spent quizzing the veteran, his employers, fellow workers, and acquaintances, there hasn't been a single word relating to the instruction. In his final report, the investigator nonetheless has the gall to urge further examination.

Surely there's no one left to query! Besides, the cost of investigation already far exceeds the pension the veteran would be receiving!

Shutting his eyes, the chief bows his grizzled head in exhaustion as much as obeisance to the Ultimate Judge: *Sylvanus served a year without evidence of disease. Doesn't that prove prior soundness? Wasn't the denial of a pension back in '62 an injustice, an injustice that the Bureau would be compounding with further delays?*

60

Floating home in a daze, Thomas practices how best to share his good news with Tillie, Little Sadie, and Baby Ellen:

I've been granted a pension.

I'm not just getting a monthly pension, but back pension as well!

The agency's won me over ten years—

"Papa's coming!"

At Little Sadie's shout, he bursts into a limping lope and hurtles into the kitchen, announcing, "We've got the money to open a laundry."

Tillie, at the stove, hoorays. Grabbing the lids off two pots, she clangs them like cymbals, singing, "No more outside work for Papa! We'll work together inside all day, every day."

Spinning like a whirligig around his legs, Little Sadie pipes, "Me, too!"

"Too," Baby Ellen, ever eager to join in, lisps.

Echoing, "Too," Tillie clatters the lids back onto the pots, and from her tone, the angular swoop of her arms, Thomas knows she's resting her hands on her swelling belly.

Little Sadie having spun to a halt, he seizes the chance to drop into a chair. Instantly, she leans against him. "Mama's wrong. We're more than two. Isn't that right, Papa?"

"*You* tell us," Thomas encourages.

As Sadie sings, "Me, Baby Ellen, Mama, Baby in Mama, Papa," she taps one finger after another on his lap so he can track her count.

Her sister toddles to each person named.

"FIVE," Little Sadie concludes triumphantly, raising her open right hand up directly in front of his face.

Baby Ellen claps, croons, "Five."

"Right you *all* are," Thomas praises, patting Little Sadie's head, sweeping Baby Ellen up in his arms, and beaming at Tillie.

~~~

To accommodate the children's eagerness to join in their enterprise, Tillie's inability to read or cipher, his poor sight, Thomas makes a game out of how to mark incoming laundry, receipts. And the resulting code of big, bold shapes, squiggles, and curlicues works faultlessly.

At their customers' puzzlement, he laughs and jokes. He wants to believe their "Lookee, lookee, Chinee laundryman!" "Chinkee, Chinkee, here my tickee," are said in good fun, too.

61

Unlike his neighbor Thomas, who shrugs off ridicule, Jackson can't, won't.

Not as a slave coming up in Virginia.

Not as a soldier fighting for freedom in the colored troops.

Not now the effects of sunstroke at Petersburg hold him captive and he's had to surrender his job of light cleaning at the lawyer's office.

Some days the omnipresent sensation of metal bands squeezing his head screw so tight he's crazed from hurting. But when the pain isn't too bad, he's still capable of reading, writing, and thinking.

Politicians, though, condescendingly dismiss his challenges to debate. And on those occasions newspapers publish his letters to the editor, he's not credited as their true author on account of they're too articulate for a Negro, in particular one with the gumption and brains to educate himself!

"Never mind white folks," his wife, Genny, soothes.

But he does mind, and he won't deny it the way his Genny does her heartache that they aren't blessed with children like their neighbors.

~~~

Thomas has taught Sadie the prayer he said nightly as a boy, and listening to her earnestly repeat the words, Little Ellen valiantly trailing a beat later, Tillie humming the *Rock-a-bye* lullaby to Eleanor May in her arms, their fourth child snug in her belly, he envisions each one learning from the older, then their children and grandchildren carrying on the tradition:

"As I lay me down to sleep,
I pray the Lord my soul to keep,
If I shall die before I wake,
I pray the Lord my soul to take."

He doesn't consider the prayer's meaning, never has, not until the morning he can't wake Little Ellen because their Lord's taken her soul.

Then it's too late.

~~~

Thomas blames himself for failing to safeguard Little Ellen from death by changing the words in the prayer, as he has in many a song. Tillie shrieks against the Almighty. Sadie cries from fear of dying herself as much as missing her sister. And Eleanor May, frightened by her mother's and Sadie's loud weeping, wails....

~~~

In snatches of broken sleep, Thomas plummets again and again to burial duty in the war.

As he drags the half-rotted corpse, flies buzz up his arms, burrow into his nostrils, ears, eyes, lips, and his hold on the ankles slackens. Tightening his grip, maggoty puss trickles over his fingers. Skin slips from flesh, flesh from bone—

Jerking upright in bed, Thomas hurtles into the greater horror of his little Ellen crushed and decaying under six feet of dirt; Tillie soak-

ing the pillow beside his with her sobbing; Eleanor May howling between them; Sadie screaming.

~~~

Genny will forever mourn the children she and her James can't
have, so she reckons it natural Tillie can't stop crying for her dead
daughter.

But *any* ruckus splashes like kerosene on the fire that sunstroke
lit in Jacksons's head at Petersburg, and since Tillie and the children
have stopped going to the laundry, there's *no* relief day or night from
their wild keening.

62

Genny, failing to quiet her neighbors with pleas, reports Tillie to the High Constable for disturbing the peace. But he refuses to accept a complaint from a colored woman about a white.

Desperate to douse Jackson's fire, Genny draws buckets of cool water for soaking sheets that she wraps tight around his flailing limbs, rags she folds into compresses and applies to his sizzling-hot head.

Fast as the cloths warm, she replaces them with fresh, all the while praying they'll tame his agony, prevent his skull from shattering, else he'll turn to demon whiskey, do something foolish.

~~~

If any veteran threatened him, Thomas would shrug it off, pretending he didn't hear, and he feels a special kinship to Jackson who also ran from slavery and was felled by war injuries as hidden and severe as his.

But no matter how extenuating the circumstances, how many or heartrending the pleas from Genny for understanding, Thomas won't overlook a threat to his family.

"It's my duty to protect them, and I've already lost one child. I can't fail my wife and children again."

~~~

COMPLAINT

INDIANA COUNTY

COMMONWEALTH OF PENNSYLVANIA

This 25th Day of November, A.D., 1882, before George Row, a
Justice of the Peace in Indiana, personally came Thomas Sylvanus,
who, upon oath, doth depose and say, that on the 21st day of November, A.D., 1882, a certain James Jackson, colored, did make threats to
shoot the child of affiant and that by reason of said threats affiant fears
injury may be done his child by said James Jackson.

Complainant therefore desires and prays for a warrant to issue,
and that the aforesaid James Jackson may be arrested and held to answer said charge.

~~~

Indiana Democrat
December 21, 1882
Com. vs. James Jackson. Surety of
the peace. Thos. Sylvanus, pros.
True bill.

~~~

Angrily crumpling the *Democrat*, Genny stuffs it into the stove
and, like the paper scorching atop the red-hot coals, she smolders,
crackles into flame.

What kind of justice is it when they arrest and find guilty someone
good but damaged, damaged and driven mad!

~~~

233

Thomas understands that Genny can't accept either his complaint or the verdict any more than he could her husband's threats. To his prayers for his family's restoration, though, he adds, *Ease Jackson's and Genny's pain, too. Help us return to good neighbors.*

63

For agonizing months, Thomas feared for Tillie's sanity. "There's no going back," he told her over and over. "Only forward." Still, she tearfully pleaded to rename Eleanor May "Little Ellen." Finally, she acceded to a compromise: Little Ella. Then came the new baby he named for Sister John who saved him from the dead cart in Andersonville. Of course, Baby John couldn't take the place of their lost girl. No child ever will. But his sunny gurgling has lessened Tillie's weeping, which has quieted Little Ella. And Sadie, beginning school, is brightening from the pleasure of lessons.

Nights, now, Thomas listens to her recite a new, carefully considered prayer he's taught her, one directed to the Savior:

"Thank you, Jesus, for another day,

The chance to learn,

The chance to play;

And as I lay me down to sleep,

Please guard me, Jesus, through the night,

Keep me safe till morning's light."

Little Ella and Baby John, too, Thomas adds, tucking them into bed and cradle, listening for their breathing to even, deepen into slumber.

Regular as pickets, he and Tillie rise through the night to check on the children: Sadie first, then Little Ella, Baby John. As he reaches down to rest the flat of his hand on a little chest, Tillie's arm on his tenses. His is no less taut. Feeling a steady rise and fall, relief flashes in him; her arm on his relaxes. Their every muscle tightens for the next.

All three safe, he offers a silent, fervent prayer of thanks, returns to bed with Tillie. Lying side by side, he senses her drifting into thin, fitful sleep. Lest he disturb her, he wills himself to keep still despite roiling over their future.

Tillie's not returned to the laundry. At the very suggestion, she chokes, "Little Ellen was so happy there," erupts in renewed grief.

But without Tillie's eyes, he misses stains, wrinkles, missing buttons, and he's failing to win back customers lost during the maelstrom. More are leaving....

~~~

In the schoolyard, children call her a bastard, but Sadie doesn't care. She'd rather be with Papa, even though the laundry without Mama and Little Ellen makes her sad.

There are so few customers that there are still some laundry tickets Little Ellen helped make. How much fun they used to have cutting paper into six-inch squares, mixing lamp-black with water for ink, joining in Papa's songs, laughing with Mama at his jokes!

Yesterday Papa said in a scary whisper, "Sadie girl, we're going to lose the laundry."

He must have been teasing. A laundry's too big to lose!

But he looked so unhappy, she couldn't crack a smile.

And when she repeated his words to Papa's friend, Uncle Manny, and asked if it was a joke, he shook his head no.

~~~

Manny understands loss. At the start of the war, five childhood friends enlisted with him, and all were killed during a charge in which a jagged fragment from a whistling rebel shell hacked off his left ear, cheekbone, and jaw, carrying away half his teeth.

Since *he* avoids looking in the glass, finds his thick utterances nigh incomprehensible and the accompanying wet sprays repellant, Manny doesn't blame anyone, kin or stranger, for dodging him.

But he prizes the select fraternity that neither shrinks nor flinches nor makes excuses for hasty departures and struggle to understand him. So he laboriously reminds Thomas how often in the war they got pummeled, retreated, regrouped. "Shut down this laundry. Give Tillie a year or two, then open in a new location, and I'll wager the two of you will have another success."

FRATERNITY
1885 – 1887

Indiana County,
Pennsylvania

Rayne
Township

Cherry Hill
Township

Indiana Borough

White
Township

64

Indiana Democrat
March 5, 1885
Thomas Sylvanus, our Christianized
China man, has opened a Laundry on Water street, opposite the
Gompers Hotel, and claims that
he can do the work as well as any
city laundry. Give Tom a chance
and encourage 'home industry.'

~~~

At the announcement for Thomas's and Tillie's return to the laundry business, Manny hastens to show support by bundling together a
wash—discovers they've only had a trickle of customers.

The paper should have reminded readers that Thomas isn't an or-
dinary Christianized China man; he's a stout-hearted Yankee!

Huh, a bronze star hanging from a small chiffon flag pinned to
Thomas's chest would bring him customers faster than a buzz saw can
turn; and, as a Grand Army of the Republic comrade in good standing,
Manny aims to make it happen by chowder.

According to the rules, a GAR comrade can sponsor for membership any honorably discharged officer or enlisted man, colored or

white, from the army or navy. But every comrade in Indiana's Post #23 is white, and a single nay vote puts the kibosh on a candidate's acceptance. Moreover, Thomas can't pay the three dollars muster-in fee, fifty cents for dues, and sixty cents for a badge.

So Manny doesn't add his mangled blather, gushers worthy of a nor'easter to the challenge. Instead, he spells out an irresistible proposal to the post commandant:

Sponsor Thomas Sylvanus, 81st Pennsylvania Infantry for membership and waive muster-in fee, dues, and cost of badge.

In exchange, we will get bragging rights, the honor of being the sole GAR post in the nation with a full-fledged China man.

65

Indiana News
May __, 1885

Tuesday was a gala day for the
G.A.R. boys in Indiana. Comrades
from other posts, viz, Saltsburg,
Blairsville, Mechanicsburg, Marion,
Cherrytree, Philadelphia, Pittsburg,
and even New York came to witness
the Department Commander's
inspection of Post 28 and muster-
in two recruits: Thomas Sylvanus,
the only naturalized Chinaman in
the U.S. army, and our well known
merchant, G.T. Hamilton.
At the conclusion of these ceremonies, the comrades wended their
way out of the hall from whence
they took up the line of march
preceded by the Indiana cornet band
for the Armory Hall where invited
dignitaries and guests waited to
help eat beans and hardtack.

~~~

Sadie races to the new laundry after school, but before going in, she likes to reread the newspaper clipping of Papa's muster-in that Uncle Manny pasted on the window.

Already there are so many customers she steps into a fog of warm steam as thick as in their old place, and every day, Papa and Mama are welcoming more. Whether they're stirring giant pots of wash with big wooden ladles, hunched over the washboard scrubbing stubborn stains, or clanking cooled irons back onto the stove, picking up hot, Papa's singing, Mama humming along. Usually Little Ella's silent except for the snip-snip of her scissors because sticking out her tongue helps stop her hands from wobbling while cutting squares for laundry tickets; Baby John's napping in a soft heap of waiting wash.

Sorting the heap into smaller piles of whites, colored, darks, Sadie's careful not to disturb him. Sometimes, though, her nose tickles from a smelly article, and she sneezes, which makes her laugh. Then Mama and Papa join in. Little Ella puts down scissors and paper so she can, too. And at her giggles, Baby John babbles so funnily in his sleep, they all laugh even harder.

66

With the laundry doing a rip-roaring trade, Thomas can't deny his family the pleasure of meat on the table, the children new shoes, Tillie pretty ribbons. But honor demands he repay his accumulated debts, too, and to his dismay, he can't scrape together fifty cents for his GAR dues. Yet he owes his plenty *to* the GAR.

Manny, gesticulating wildly, dismisses the dues, reminds in a string of explosive wet splutters that the GAR motto is loyalty, honor, and charity, not grudging, purse-lipped, hand-out charity, but a comradely helping hand.

Camaraderie really *is* at the core of the GAR, Thomas realizes. Every member, whether he served as an officer or enlisted man, holds the rank of comrade, and his poverty or wealth and social standing as a civilian makes no difference within the post. So at weekly campfires, he—a laundryman—is as likely to be jammed cheek by jowl alongside a laborer as a carriage maker, teacher, judge, farmer, brick layer, or senator, offering him an opportunity to ensure another deserving veteran receives long overdue recognition.

~~~

At weekly campfires, Harry White enjoys recounting his many thwarted attempts to escape from Andersonville, his eventual success

245

due to courageous darkies who risked brutal punishment to secrete him by day, pilot him by night.

Indebted to those selfless souls, he battled successfully as a senator in the Pennsylvania Senate for the Negroes' right to equal protection as well as suffrage; and since GAR rules forbid outside business, including politics, in a post's hall, no comrade's ever breathed a word about it at campfires. But back when the laws passed, many of these same comrades expressed their anger elsewhere, and to avoid riling them anew, he's deliberately ignored his pricks of conscience over the post's lack of a single veteran from a colored regiment.

Now, asked by Tom Chinaman to sponsor James Jackson, Sixth U.S. Colored Infantry, for membership, Harry floods with shame, gives ready agreement. Then, utilizing the same strategies that worked in the senate for quelling grumblings, outright rebellion, he battles for the trooper's approval.

~~~

For Jackson, his GAR badge shines like the North Star that guided runaways to freedom.

How hard he fought for an end to slavery.

How loud he shouted jubilee at victory!

How galling the exclusion of every single colored regiment from the celebratory two-day Grand Review of Union Armies in Washington.

Despite his many letters to the committees charged with organizing the borough's observance of Decoration Day each May, no orator has ever acknowledged the service of colored regiments; no colored—not even Thomas, who fought in white outfits—has ever been invited to march in the procession of veterans and fraternal organizations to decorate the graves of war dead with flowers.

This year, though, the glittering GAR badges pinned to their chests guarantee their inclusion, and Jackson proudly steps into the ranks beside the Chinese Yankee.

67

Sadie prickles with delicious goosebumps. She thought nothing could top cheering Papa, Uncle Manny, and Uncle Jackson in the grand Decoration Day procession. But Papa's been invited to give a talk at the Court House, the very place where *hundreds* gather outside for speeches before the procession. And although it will be a school night for her and Ella and way past Little John's bedtime, Papa says Mama can bring all of them to hear him.

~~~

Indiana Progress
February 24, 1887
The lecture of Ah Yee Way, at the
Court House, on last Monday
evening was listened to by a small
audience. Ah Yee Way, better known
as Thomas Sylvanus, is the only
Chinaman known ever to have
been a soldier in the United States
Army. The lecturer briefly told of
his birth and early life; his immi-
gration to America at ten years of

age; his witnessing the Baltimore riot on the 19th of April, 1861, on the occasion of the march of Gen. Butler's Massachusetts soldiers through that city to the relief of Washington, his enlistment, army experience, capture, and ten months imprisonment at Andersonville. The talk was very entertaining through-out and merited a much larger audi-ence. Ah Yee Way desires us in this connection to express his thanks to the persons who attended his unpre-tentious talk and also to the Indiana Cornet Band for music furnished prior to the lecture.

UNION
1888 - 1890

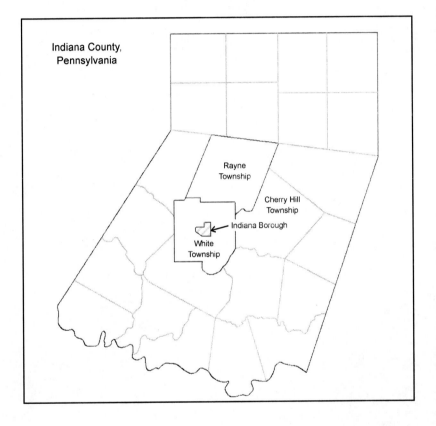

Indiana County,
Pennsylvania

Rayne
Township

Cherry Hill
Township

Indiana Borough

White
Township

68

Thomas marks his sharp decline—and the laundry's—from the chill he caught last winter.

It developed into a bout of bronchitis that reopened the sores on his leg, laming him until he couldn't rise from bed at all and Tillie was so consumed by his care that for weeks, she never got to the laundry. Of course, they lost customers, and although he's recovered enough to work again, only the most loyal have returned.

Now he's got to move his family to a street with poor drainage and quarrelsome inhabitants, chief among them James P. George, a lardy, loud-mouthed pump maker....

~~~

James P. George isn't about to hush. What he's got to say is too important.

America's for white men. Yes, it is. *Born* Yankees, not pretenders like that chink-nigger laundryman.

Furthermore, *all* pretenders should be chased out of the borough the way honest Yankee-born workingmen over in Blacklick ran the Italians out of the brickworks, then the township. Their wives and spawn, too.

~~~

Clamping starched collars in the striking machine, Sadie pretends she's squishing Mr. George, who yells at her and Ella whenever he knows Papa can't leave the house because the big purple sores on his lame leg hurt too much.

Huh, that coward better watch out!

If he doesn't shut his mouth, she'll punch him like she does schoolyard bullies that call her a bastard or Ella ching-chong-ching while slanting their eyes with their fingers!

~~~

Ella wishes Sadie would let her tell Papa about mean Mr. George barreling out of his pump shop, shaking his fist, and hollering threats.

Sadie says, "We mustn't worry Papa. He's got to rest so he can get well. Besides, Mr. George can't catch us."

She even jeers, "Ha, ha, Fatty can't run," at him as they take off, and he does waddle slow as a pig. But Mr. George could trap them like he does in nightmares.

Papa would stop the bullying, and soon as he's well enough to get out of bed, I'll tell him no matter what Sadie says.

69

Emerging from days and weeks lost to fever, Thomas learns the laundry is lost, his family scraping by with the help of the GAR. Surely the Bureau of Pensions will grant him a full pension now for his eyes *and* leg.

~~~

The doctor fumes at Washington's willingness to pour money into waging war, refusal to fund treatment for veterans. Had Thomas received surgery, he'd not be reduced to discerning mere light and shadows. Nor would his leg be studded from knee to ankle with crippling eruptions of periosteal ulceration so painful he breaks out in sweats.

The government's criteria for granting pensions further betray the men who helped save it! Despite years of appeals, Thomas *still* only receives a partial pension for his eyes, nothing for his leg.

Clearly nobody in the War Department recalls the chaos of battle or staggering numbers of men killed in action, else they'd credit the veteran's explanation for why there's no record of treatment for his injury at Cold Harbor and accept that the sole witness to his fall was killed in the rifle pits at Petersburg.

Even the most frugal veteran couldn't support himself, let alone a family of five, on a partial pension for cataracts, and Thomas is forced to hawk vegetables and fruit in all weathers. He hides his lameness by leaning on the cart he pushes to his post outside the Court House. He identifies friends and acquaintances from their voices, makes change by touch. There's no smothering his wracking wet coughs, however.

70

Leaving Tillie to mind their vegetable and fruit cart, Little John to make change, Thomas leans heavily on his brave girls and begins his wheezy ascent up the courthouse steps.

At each shaky footfall, a lightning bolt of pain shoots from leg through spine; the truth of his son's innocent, "Mama, Papa is broken like Humpty Dumpty," pierces his heart. Still he labors up the next step, then another. *How dare that cowardly James George strike my Sadie and Ella, get that snake of a High Constable to refuse my complaint! Did those villains think I'd let an assault on my children slide because it's not in the constabularies' quarterly report to the court?*

~~~

COMPLAINT
INDIANA COUNTY
COMMONWEALTH OF PENNSYLVANIA

On this 18th day of August, A.D., 1888, before George Row, a Justice of the Peace in and for Indiana County, came Thomas Sylvanus who, sworn according to the law, deposes that on this day, as he is informed and verily believes, a certain James P. George did commit an assault and battery upon Sadie Sylvanus and Ella Sylvanus, children of the affiant, by striking and beating them. Wherefore affiant desires that said James P. George be arrested and held to answer said charge.

~~~

Indiana Weekly Messenger
September 19, 1888
The case of the Com. Vs James P. George was tried. It seems that Thomas Sylvanus, the Chinaman, lives near the defts. store; his children have been annoying the deft. and he chastised them; this angered Thomas and he rushed to seek protection of the laws of his adopted land. There was a good deal of evidence about family quarrels. The jury considered it all and concluded that Mr. George was guilty enough to pay 2/3 of the costs and Sylvanus the other 1/3 and so returned.

~~~

The verdict wasn't the solid indictment Thomas sought. But even with the conscienceless pump maker and his cronies heaping lies upon lies from the witness stand, the truth wasn't completely defeated. *I'm not either. I can yet protect my family, and I will!*

71

Fever flushed yet clammy, Thomas shivers from the winter storm raging outside, the wind whistling into the house through gaping cracks, the doctor's latest diagnosis: The drenching sweats aren't just from pain nor the chest congestions mere chronic bronchitis, but deadly tuberculosis.

His every breath a labored swoosh and gurgle broken by bone-rattling hacking, his ruined eyes and injured leg battering rams of hurt, Death doesn't frighten. What scoops out his insides is losing Tillie and the children, their abandonment.

Sadie has always been bold, Ella skittish. John's tougher. Only six, though, he's as vulnerable as Ah Yee Way was to Mrs. McClintock. They all are: After the death of a comrade that the GAR has been supporting, the Women's Relief Corps, every one of whom exhibits Mrs. McClintock's absolute certitude, takes charge of the family left behind. Sweet, biddable Tillie will be crushed, their children—

Thomas chokes back the awful possibilities.

If only he could be sure the Bureau of Pensions will grant them the pensions for widows and orphans. Then he'd know his family safe, and he could rest. But he can't. So, skewered in pain, he keeps fighting for one more ragged breath, another, with Tillie applying a hot mustard plaster to his chest; Sadie salving his sores; Ella, her little hand quivering in his; John's sticky fingers clutching his the way Ah Yee Way did the kindly sailor....

EPILOGUE

Thomas Sylvanus died at 2 a.m. June 15, 1891. GAR Post #28 took charge of his funeral and attended in a body.

As Thomas feared, the GAR Women's Relief Corps soon coerced Tillie into surrendering the two younger children for placement in Soldiers' Orphan Schools. She never received a pension, and although the broken family struggled to reunite, they never succeeded.

Almost a hundred years after Thomas's death, Richard G. Hoover, a Vietnam veteran and Civil War re-enactor whose great-grandfathers fought in the conflict, came across the weathered headstone in Indiana's Oakland Cemetery. The engraving was barely decipherable. When he brought it to the attention of the John T. Crawford Post, Camp 43 of the Sons of Union Veterans of the Civil War, they arranged for the headstone to be replaced.

Regulations only allowed for one regiment to be engraved on the stone, which was rededicated on July 10, 2005.

A HISTORICAL NOTE

In the nineteenth century, Westerners always viewed the removal of children from China as benevolent regardless of whether they were orphaned. Either due to their youth or the trauma of removal, these children often retained minimal and confused memories of their origins. Of his early years, Ah Yee Way could only remember leaving Hong Kong for school in Pennsylvania with Mrs. McClintock; "falling into the hands" of Dr. Sylvanus Mills, who turned him over to his sister, Mary Duvall; choosing the name of Thomas to honor "the kindly sailor;" baptism as Thomas Sylvanus Duvall; witnessing the Baltimore riot; and then running away to enlist in Philadelphia.

There were three categories for race in the 1860 census—White, Black, or Mulatto—and how a Chinese was identified fluctuated. Thomas was consistently described as dark complexioned. The census enumerator in Baltimore expressed his puzzlement over Thomas's appropriate designation by making something akin to an exclamation mark. Nor could subsequent enumerators categorize him more definitively.*

Encounters with Chinese were rare in the eastern states. But most children read the popular *Peter Parley's Universal History* that described Chinese as rat-and-dog-eating liars addicted to cheating. Period magazines were also rife with negative images. Chinese displayed in tours sponsored by P. T. Barnum or missionaries generally projected more positive yet no less stereotypic images.

That Thomas nonetheless won acceptance, admiration, and respect in White regiments can be attributed to his character as well as the nature of a soldier's small, tight-knit community where men depended on each other for survival, not just on battlefields, but when on grueling marches, felled by sickness, or captured as prisoners of war. Many Union veterans sought to preserve this camaraderie through membership in the Grand Army of the Republic and participation in a post's weekly campfires.

Although Thomas and his GAR post believed him the only Chinese who served in the Union army, he was not. Readers interested in learning more about Chinese in the U.S. Civil War will find additional information on my website www.mccunn.com and the National Park Service publication *Asians and Pacific Islanders and the Civil War.*

~~~

I reclaimed Thomas's life from census schedules; military, court, and tax records; pension files; archival documents; reminiscences; newspapers; journals; and local histories.

Except for a few instances of irregular punctuation and excess verbiage, I did not change any of the documents or newspaper clippings in the body of the novel. Besides Thomas, I obtained the pension file for his widow, Tillie Askins Sylvanus, and the military record and pension file for James Jackson, Sixth U.S. Colored Troops.

For clarity, I used surname alone for James Mahan, Christian names only for Tillie and the children. I could not find a Christian name for Mrs. McClintock or Reverend Alexander. Otherwise, all characters drawn from historical records have their complete names.

I did not alter the trajectory of Thomas's life that research uncovered, but my findings, while rich in incident and clues to his character, yielded no direct personal reflections. So for context, understanding, and analysis, I turned to the letters, diaries, and reminiscences of contemporaries, as well as scholarly works in diverse areas.

The sole extant reminiscence of a Chinese American Civil War veteran is by Hong Neok Woo, who served in the Fiftieth Regiment of the Pennsylvania Ninety-Day Emergency Militia (typescript, edited by Y. Y. Tsu, Archives of the Episcopal Church, Austin, Texas, 1915). Woo's experiences, like the lives of other Chinese Civil War veterans, offered insights into Thomas's as well as a lens through which to read the accounts of non-Chinese. John Kuo Wei Tchen's *New York before Chinatown: Orientalism & the Shaping of American Culture 1776-1882* (Johns Hopkins University Press, 1999) provided helpful context.

Thomas's precarious position between slave and freedmen, Black and White, in Maryland, the Union Army, and Pennsylvania was brought home to me by the following works: Ralph Clayton's *Slavery, Slaveholding, and the Free Black Population of Antebellum Baltimore* (Heritage Books, 1993); Barbara Jeanne Fields' *Slavery and Freedom on the Middle Ground: Maryland during the Nineteenth Century* (Yale University Press, 1985); James M. McPherson's *The Negro's Civil War: How American Blacks Felt and Acted During the War for the Union* (Ballantine, 1991); Frank H. Taylor's *Philadelphia in the Civil War 1861-1865* (The City, 1913); J. Matthew Gallman's *Mastering Wartime: A Social History of Philadelphia during the Civil War* (Cambridge University Press, 1990); Sonya Stewart's Master's thesis "Working Together: African American Migration and Settlement in Indiana County, Pennsylvania" (Indiana University of Pennsylvania, 1996); Clarence D. Stephenson's four volume *Indiana County 175th Anniversary History* (A. G. Haldin Publishing Company, 1978); and Wayne Smith's *The Price of Patriotism: Indiana County, Pennsylvania and the Civil War* (Burd Street Press, 1998).

Critical to my understanding Thomas's repeated enlistments and the broad range of commitment and opposition to the war among soldiers were: *What They Fought For 1861-1865* by James W. McPherson (Louisiana State University Press, 1994); *Embattled Courage: The Experience of Combat in the American Civil War* by Gerald F. Linderman (Free Press, 1987); *Heroes & Cowards: The Social Face of War* by Dora L. Costa and Matthew E. Kahn (Princeton University Press, 2008); and *A People's History of the Civil War: Struggles for the Meaning of Freedom* by David Williams (New Press, 2005).

No regimental histories exist for the three in which Thomas served. For the campaigns in which he fought, I relied on the three-volume *The Army of the Potomac* by Bruce Catton (Doubleday, 1952). His service in the Eighty-first Pennsylvania Voluntary Infantry coincided with Colonel Charles F. Johnson, whose detailed letters to his wife have been published in *The Civil War Letters of Colonel Charles F. Johnson, Invalid Corps*, edited with an introduction by Fred Pelka (University of Massachusetts Press, 2004.) The description of the regiment's training camp came from Ruth Harvey Schaeffer's Masters thesis, "Certain Aspects of Life in Easton, Pennsylvania during the Civil War." The gruesome work of the Fifty-first Regiment Infantry, Pennsylvania Ninety-Day Militia, 1863, is from *A Strange and Blighted Land, Gettysburg: The Aftermath of a Battle* by Gregory A. Coco (Thomas Publications, 1995). The only direct source for the Forty-second New York Voluntary Infantry was a pamphlet *Union Forever: under Two Flags* by Philip Kreis. Very helpful, however, were the illustrated diaries of Private Robert Knox Sneden, 40th New York Infantry, published in *Eye of the Storm: A Civil War Odyssey* edited by Charles F. Bryan, Jr. & Nelson D. Lankford (The Free Press, 2000). Fortuitously, I stumbled upon the capture at the Weldon Railroad and journey to Andersonville in *A Casualty at Gettysburg and Anderson-*

ville: Selections from the Civil War Diary of Private Austin A. Carr of the 82nd N.Y. Infantry edited by David G. Martin (Longstreet House).

The heartbreaking diaries of Andersonville's prisoners made the stockade come alive for me, but without William Marvel's *Andersonville: the Last Depot* (University of North Carolina Press, 2006), I'd have become lost in their contradictions and biases. Nor would I have understood Thomas's transfer to Millen, return, hospitalization, and final confusing weeks as prisoner.

The hospital in which Thomas was hospitalized in 1862 had unique features which I learned about in Dr. Sandra W. Moss's "To Treat War's 'Wounded and Diseased,' Newark's Civil War Hospital" (New Jersey State Archives).

Stuart McConnell's *Glorious Contentment: The Grand Army of the Republic, 1865-1900* (University of North Carolina Press, 1997) provided the key to understanding Thomas's membership in Indiana's Post #23.

For how Americans then voted, I relied on Richard Franklin Bensel's *The American Ballot Box in the Mid-Nineteenth Century* (Press Syndicate of the University of Cambridge, 2004).

The sole extant image of anyone in the Sylvanus family is a morgue photograph of Thomas's son, John. Though poor, it aided in the selection and creation of the cover image.

To help me sort through the many contradictions and outright errors in the historical records of Thomas's life, I consulted many additional sources (see Acknowledgments).

The responsibility for my ultimate choices, their portrayal, and the interpretation of Thomas's internal life in *Chinese Yankee* is mine—as are any errors.

* By 1870, Chinese and Indian had been added to the racial categories, and the enumerator wrote, "China" for Thomas's place of birth, but in the column for Color, there's a "b" that has been slashed through firmly. In 1880, the enumerator clearly marked Thomas's wife and children as "W," but his race is a smudge of indecisive second guessing. In the summaries at www.ancestry.com, Thomas's race in the 1870 census is "Black;" in 1880, "Chinese."

ACKNOWLEDGMENTS

Chinese Yankee owes its existence to the generous assistance of many.

From start to finish, my husband Don made the impossible possible—as he does in every aspect of my life.

Gordon Kwok, Association to Commemorate the Chinese Serving in the American Civil War, and Will Radell, Sons of Union Veterans of the Civil War, introduced me to Thomas Sylvanus. Will shared information he had recovered, and until he left Indiana, continued to research Thomas's life on my behalf at the Historical and Genealogical Society of Indiana County and Indiana University of Pennsylvania.

When Gay Chow and Alan Baumler at the University invited me to Indiana, Eleanor Mannikka made me welcome in her uniquely peaceful home. Will returned to take me to Thomas's grave and familiarize me with the borough. He gave me the photograph in the Epilogue.

The able assistance of Coleen Chambers, Pat Johner, and Coralie Hershman made it possible for me to scour the Historical Society's rich resources despite my limited time. Wonderfully helpful on location and via email were Theresa R. McDevitt, Rhonda Yeager, Indiana University Library; Marc Morrison, Lauri Steffy, Indiana Public Library; Kathy Dean, Office of the Prothonotary. Interviews with Chris Catalfamo, Irwin Marcus, and Rick Essenwein gave me context, as did Sonya Barclay's amazing dissertation "Reading the Social Landscape: A Lexicon of Rural Class in Western Pennsylvania 1790-

1860" (Carnegie Mellon, 2008). Sonya Stewart's insights, suggestions, and encouragement through the years have been as invaluable as her groundbreaking research on Indiana County's African American Community 1850-1880.

In digging out valuable information from dusty, crumbling paper records, Richard Hoover has no peer. His generosity, commitment to Thomas, and passion for the history of Indiana County and the Civil War shine.

The recovery of any Civil War veteran's service must begin with a search for military and pension records at the National Archives. Dennis Michael Edelin, Supervisor Archives Specialist, was always helpful when questions arose, as were Juliette Arai and De Anne Blanton. The late Ed Milligan's assistance in looking up veterans' records at the archives will forever be missed.

I owe my "military training" to Irving Moy, President, Co.F, 14th Connecticut Voluntary Infantry and his gifts of August V. Kautz's *The 1865 Customs of Service for Non-commissioned Officers and Soldiers* (Stackpole, 2001), *Hardee's Rifle and Light Infantry Tactics* (J.O. Kane, 1862), *The Columbia Rifles Research Compendium, Second Edition,* compiled and edited by John E. Tobey (Watchdog Quarterly, Inc., 2006). Irving's kind patience as a teacher is incomparable. Insisting on the importance of my personally walking the battlefields, he tempted me with maps and literature until I succumbed.

Rangers, historians, and curators at every site enthusiastically shared their knowledge, including: Walton H. Owen, Fort Ward Museum; Randy Washburn, Spotsylvania; Randy Cleaver, Richmond; John Heiser, Howard O. Frankenfield, and Clyde R. Bell, Gettysburg.

Doc Gillespie at the former Libby Prison explained the processing of captured soldiers. Angela Clark at Andersonville sent a cornucopia of information. Michael J. Olson, Gallaudet University Archives, provided the details about the military encampment at Kendall Green. In other matters military, I'm indebted to Christopher Morton, Curator, and Jim Gandy, archivist, New York State Military Museum; Jason L. Wilson, Research Historian, Pennsylvania Capitol Preservation Committee; Ted Dombroski and Scott Kuchta, re-enactors in the 81st Pennsylvania Voluntary Infantry.

I was incredibly fortunate to have the insightful counsel of Eddie Fung, the sole Chinese in his military unit and a longtime prisoner of war in World War II. Pat Steenland, Corliss Lee, and Teresa Salazar smoothed my transition to the world of online research. Debbie Wei and Vera DaVinci got me to Philadelphia; Vera's warm hospitality gave me needed time in the city; her introductions opened doors.

Richard Saylor, Pennsylvania State Archives, directed me to Bob Felten, Western Pennsylvania Genealogical Society, who found the documentation for Thomas's citizenship, including the clerk's entry of "Ireland" in the "Nativity" column.

Layne Bosserman, Enoch Pratt Free Library, recovered the marriage, birth, death dates and more for members of the Duvall family. She directed me to the work of Ralph Clayton which identified Mrs. Duvall as a slaveholder. Also helpful was Christopher Busta-Peck.

At the San Francisco Public Library, Janice Torbet tracked down invaluable information with dogged enthusiasm and success; Ron Romano again located and obtained essential material through interlibrary loan; Jerry Dear repeatedly, yet patiently, saved me from my ineptitude in looping microfilm. At my local branch, I could count on the cheerful and helpful support of Carol Small and Lourdes Fortunada.

Crucial information also came from: Barbara Walcott; Blegen Library, University of Cincinnati; Sharon Gothard, Easton Area Public Library; Corliss Lee, Moffitt Library, University of California, Berkeley; Bette M. Epstein, New Jersey State Archives; Alice Gingold, New York Historical Society; New York Public Library; Jane S. Moyer,

Librarian, Northampton City Museum; Steven Wright, Philadelphia Free Library; Sisters of Charity, in particular S. Judith Metz; Richard Musselman; Diane Shaw, Archivist, Skillman Library, Lafayette College.

Many people generously gave crucial support, shared specific areas of expertise: Elizabeth L. Abbott, Archie Blake, Greg Bohm, Dr. Alfred Bollet, Bruce Boswell, Emmanuel Dabney, William Eng, Terry Foenander, Robin Grossman, John Hennessy, Marlon Hom, Yvette Huginnie, Betty Jung, Bob Krick, Jeff Low, Valerie Matsumoto, Charles McClain, Laurie Wu McClain, Tim McCunn, Drummond McCunn, Dr. Jeffrey Morris, Peggy Pascoe, Jack Kuo Wei Tchen, Tsoi Nuliang, Judy Yung, Rye Zemelsky.

The manuscript underwent many drafts and, at every stage, benefited from the keen insights and suggestions of readers, some of whom gave their close attention to multiple versions: Deng Ming Dao, Vera Da Vinci, Robin Grossman, Eddie Fung, Juliet Grames, Greg Holch, Richard G. Hoover, Caroline M. H. Kraus, Miriam Locke, Don McCunn, Irving Moy, Harry Nimmo, George Ow, Pat Steenland, Debbie Wei, and Judy Yung. Lynda Preston's fine editorial eye gave the manuscript final polish.

John Busovicki generously gave me permission to use the image of the Courthouse in Indiana, Pennsylvania from his private collection. Sonya Stewart sent me the image.

For the past twenty years I've enjoyed the support of Peter Ginsberg, Dave Barbor, and Laura Blake Peterson at Curtis Brown Ltd.

My greatest debt is to Thomas and his family who lived this story. Chinese Yankee is for all of you, with my heartfelt thanks.